P9-DDY-545

Meditations
on the Good News

READING THE BIBLE
FOR TODAY

Rev. Debra W. Haffner

RELIGIOUS INSTITUTE

For information:
Religious Institute, Inc.
21 Charles Street, Suite 140
Westport, CT 06880
E-mail: info@religiousinstitute.org

ISBN: 978-0-9855949-1-6

Manuscript preparation: Blanca Godoi
Editing: J. Michael Cobb and Marisa Procopio
Design: Alan Barnett Design

Dedication

This book is dedicated to Marie Alford-Harkey, Michael Cobb, and Blanca Godoi, and the hundreds of members of the Religious Institute's Phoenix Circle who allowed me to believe that joy comes in the morning.

Table of Contents

INTRODUCTION

This book began with a crossword puzzle. The clue for 46 Down was "What the Bible says every person is." It had six letters. "Divine" and "worthy" didn't fit the other letters I had already filled in the Across spaces. "Sacred" didn't fit either, although the "s" was right. "Holy" was too short. "Blessed" was one letter too long. "A child of God" was much too long.

I continued to work the Across clues. An "n" appeared in 46 Down. Then "er" at the end. I realized the answer was "sinner."

I stopped, stunned. Yes, many people today—and too many theologians from St. Augustine to Aquinas to Calvin to modern day doomsayers—have taught that human nature is sinful. But as a Unitarian Universalist minister and a relatively new student of the Bible, it's not how I understand what the Bible says about humankind or the state of the world.

The idea that all people are sinners comes from the story of the Fall in Genesis 3. Because Adam and Eve ate the fruit from the tree of the knowledge of good and evil when God told them not to, some Christian theologians and clergy have taught through the ages that we are inherently sinful.

In a story that I first heard in divinity school, President Calvin Coolidge went to church alone one Sunday when Mrs. Coolidge was home ill. When he came home, she asked, "What was the sermon about?" "Sin," said the terse President. She persisted, "But what did the minister say about it?" He answered, "He was against it."

Now, it's important to tell you that I come to the Bible as a relative newcomer. I grew up in a secular Jewish household. I knew about the Ten Commandments and I was familiar with the story of the Exodus told at the Passover Seder. Like many Jewish children, my exposure to the New Testament didn't go much beyond the Christmas birth story and an image of Jesus nailed to a cross. I had never actually read the Bible from Genesis to Revelations until I was called to the ministry in my forties. I didn't think it had much to offer me in my 21st-century life, and I was certainly not interested in a worldview that labeled all people sinners.

Indeed, I wasn't different than many other people in the United States. Although almost all Christian and Jewish homes say there is a Bible in their home, two-thirds of people in polls say that they haven't read it in the past year (or probably longer). And many are woefully ignorant about what the Bible does say; most people can only list a few of the Ten Commandments when asked, and in one poll, one in ten Americans said that Joan of Arc was Noah's wife!

I loved my scripture classes in seminary as I began to study for the Unitarian Universalist ministry. It was a wonderful surprise to discover when I started reading the Bible that yes, one can find a condemning/punishing/ humans-are-sinful God, but that the opposite is true as well. As I began studying Scripture, I felt joy to learn that the Bible has hundreds of passages in which God is delighted with us. It is replete with messages that life is to be enjoyed here and now and not just in heaven, and inspirational and practical lessons to help us lead a joyful, pleasurable and easier life. I discovered more than fifteen years ago that the Bible had lessons to teach me today.

Indeed, now as a minister who has studied the Bible and loves its stories and history, I believe that it is primarily a book about love and hope. At its core, if the Bible is to speak to us today and if more people are to read it, what is needed is another look at what it says about how to celebrate our lives. We need not limit ourselves to a narrow view of the texts but instead ask how they can help us expand our lives today.

You don't need to be Christian or Jewish or Unitarian Universalist or attend a church or synagogue to benefit from these Biblical insights. You don't need to believe in a creed, or indeed believe in organized religion at all to apply these lessons in your own daily life. It doesn't matter if you read the Bible literally or as metaphor, because both types of readers can be inspired by its passages. You can be "spiritual, not religious" or "religious and spiritual" and still find or make meaning. In these pages, I offer you both my own insights and questions that may guide you to find yourself in these verses.

I hope that people who have never read the Bible — or only have the faintest memories of Bible stories from their childhood — will find inspiration within these pages. I'd love you to look up these passages in the Bible, read others, and discover for yourself the optimism for our lives that Scripture contains.

The passages are arranged in the order that they appear in the Bible. Or you may just want to open to a random page and see how the passage speaks to you.

Join me on this journey to bring the Bible into your life today. Read a passage a day in order or look for a passage that speaks to what is happening in your life. Think of each passage as a small meal, a five-minute homily, or a sermon. Let your thoughts wander to where it brings you or how it might apply to your life. Ponder or pray. Make your own notes or put a passage aside for later contemplation. Let the light of the passage, its good news, live within you.

Then God said, "Let us make humankind in our image."

Genesis 1:26

The Bible opens with a joyous message. The first chapter of the first book sets the stage for the goodness of creation. God creates light on the first day; the sky on the second; the earth, the seas and fruits and vegetables on the third; the sun, moon and stars on the fourth; and the fish and birds on the fifth. By the end of the fifth day, the physical world is created in all its magnificence and all its diversity. At the end of each of the first five days, God reviews what has occurred and declares it "good."

Then on the sixth day, after creating the animals, God creates us—humans—in God's own image. And before the day is over, God surveys all that has been created and declares, "It was *very* good" (italics mine; Gen. 1:31). Adding people, created in God's image, amplified good into "very good."

What a hopeful way to begin the Scriptures. The world is full of majestic beauty, waiting for our entrance. In Hebrew we are created *tzelem elohim;* in Latin and Christian theology, it is *Imago Dei.* We are made in the image of a gracious, knowing, forgiving, blessing, fulfilling God who has instilled within us these very same characteristics to bring to earth and each other. If God is sacred and divine, then we too are sacred and divine. Each one of us is created in God's image in all of our glorious diversity. No other scripture passage tells me as strongly that our fundamental nature is not sinful, for surely that is not in the image of God. This passage says that humans are created as fundamentally spiritual and relational beings who have inherent value and worth. Surely this passage extends to all humans throughout history, not just the ones created on that sixth day.

Religious teachings differ on the nature of humankind and the concept of sin, but I am comforted by the many times in the Bible that we are told that humans are created in God's image. (See, for example, Gen. 5:1–3, Gen. 9:6, 1 Cor. 11:7, Jas. 3:9, among others). If we hold up *Imago Dei* in our everyday lives, we can understand sin as when we mistreat each other. The Biblical call reinforces that we best know God through our relationships with each other.

What if every day we treated every person we encountered with open eyes and an open heart, with the purpose of recognizing the divine within them? Just for today, try to remember that every person you meet is created in God's image. Remember that so are you.

THEREFORE A MAN LEAVES HIS FATHER AND HIS MOTHER AND CLINGS TO HIS WIFE, AND THEY BECOME ONE FLESH. AND THE MAN AND HIS WIFE WERE BOTH NAKED, AND WERE NOT ASHAMED.

Genesis 2:24–25

Thus ends the second chapter of Genesis, the second chapter in the Bible, and an alternative to the creation story in Genesis 1.

In Genesis 1, God creates humankind on the sixth day, creating a male and a female in God's image (Gen. 1:27). The very first thing God says to these new human beings? "Be fruitful and multiply" (Gen. 1:28) or in other words, "Go have sex and make babies."

Genesis 2 is believed by most Biblical historians to have been written at an earlier time than Genesis 1 and is an alternative story of the creation. After creating Adam, God recognizes that Adam needs a companion and a helper: "It is not good that the man should be alone; I will make him a helper as his partner" (Gen. 2:18). This version goes on to say that God then formed every animal and every bird, and brought them to the man, but Adam did not find among them a suitable "helper as a partner." It is only after rejecting the animals as partners that God put the man into a deep sleep, and created Woman.

7

And then the words of Genesis 2:24–25 follow. They tell us the man and the woman were naked, they engaged in sexual intercourse, and they were not ashamed of their bodies or their sexuality. Procreation is never mentioned in this version of the creation story.

What a joyful reminder of the gift of our sexuality. At the very beginning, in the Garden of Eden, humans enjoy their bodies without shame or guilt. We are made for each other, as helpers, partners and lovers.

Side by side, the very two first chapters of the Bible emphasize the equality of men and women, recognize that we need a mate who is a helper, partner and lover, and affirm sexual acts as potentially procreative, but also joyous and re-creative without procreation. At the end of the sixth day, God "saw *everything* that God had made, and indeed, it was very good" (italics mine; Gen. 1:31). Everything—including our sexuality.

These passages remind me of a moment in Alice Walker's *The Color Purple*. Shug says in response to Celie's protest to an allusion about sexual response:

> "Oh, she say. God love all them feelings. That's some of the best stuff God did. And when you know God loves 'em you enjoys 'em a lot more. You can just relax, go with everything that's going, and praise God by liking what you like.... Listen, God love everything you love—and a mess of stuff you don't."

Rather than viewing sexuality as sinful, these opening chapters of the Bible teach that sexuality is God's life-giving and life-fulfilling gift to us. Many people mistakenly believe that the Bible only contains two messages about sexuality: "Don't" and "Sex Is Only for Procreation in Marriage." The Bible's view on sexuality is much richer and more complex than most people know. Indeed, the Bible teaches that our bodies are wonderful and to be enjoyed, that there are many forms of blessed relationships and that we must not abuse or exploit this sacred gift.

For a few moments, take the time to think about what this means to you. Growing up, did you learn that your sexuality was a blessing from God to be celebrated? Or did you learn that sexual feelings were wrong, needed to be confessed and subverted? Can you open yourself to feel deep inside your bones that your sexuality is a precious gift? What would it mean for you to "be naked and not ashamed" with yourself or with your partner? What might it mean for you today?

Remember the Sabbath day, and keep it holy. Six days you shall labor and do all your work. But the seventh day is a sabbath to the Lord your God; you shall not do any work.

Exodus 20:8–10

The call to keep the Sabbath is repeated ten times in Exodus, three times each in the books of Deuteronomy and Leviticus, and mentioned in many of the books of the Prophets. It is for most of us the commandment that is most often and most easily broken. Some religious people are committed to the Sabbath; for example, many conservative or orthodox Jews observe it by walking to their synagogues, not using electricity, and spending the day in quiet prayer and reflection. Most Jehovah's Witnesses and the Amish also are strict observers of the Sabbath.

But many of us—those of us who identify as secular and those of us who are members of faith communities—rarely do. Stores that were once closed under archaic blue laws are now open, some 24/7. We carry iPhones and iPads with us throughout our weekends, checking our work emails and chatting online with colleagues. We finish up work that didn't get finished during the week, pay our bills, and do our chores around the house and in town. Sunday and Saturday for many of us are just additional days of the week.

Some of us work on Saturday and Sunday as part of our work week. By definition most clergy work on the Sabbath, offering worship services and sermons on the day of rest. Indeed, each of the four Gospels addresses the question of whether Jesus should be preaching or healing on the Sabbath, concluding in Mark 3:4 that it "is lawful to do good on the Sabbath day." Yet, surely clergy need a day of rest as well.

My dear friend and colleague, the Reverend Kathryn E. Booth, once said in a sermon, "'Remember the Sabbath and keep it holy' is not a suggestion, but a commandment, a holy command." I wonder how many of those who seek to have the Ten Commandments enshrined in public places continue to shop, work, check their email and so on each Saturday or Sunday.

I often work six days and sometimes even seven days a week. Sometimes I have to do that for several weeks on end. I have worked as many as 21 days in a row, before I reach the point where I am desperate for a day off. I have more than once in recent years found myself exhausted, burned out, and troubled by preventable health issues because of overworking myself. I have learned the hard way that I do not serve God by working to the point of exhaustion.

Observing a Sabbath is a glorious gift to us from Scripture. As it says in Exodus 23:12, we need a day off so we "may be refreshed." The Bible passage continues in the Ten Commandments that even God needed to rest: "For in six days the Lord made heaven and earth, the sea, and all that is in them, and rested on the seventh day. Therefore the Lord blessed the Sabbath day and consecrated it" (Exod. 20:11). Or as a popular print advertisement once said, "Even God took off one day a week."

I resonate to these words from poet and storyteller E.B. White: "But I arise in the morning torn between a desire to save the world and a desire to savor the world. This makes it hard to plan the day." We all need at least a day a week just to savor the world.

Taking at least one day off for refreshment, rest and renewal is vital to our health and well being. It doesn't have to be the weekend if your working hours routinely include Saturday or Sunday; Sabbath can take place just as well on Tuesday or Thursday. What is important is to take the time to unplug from technology, step back from our work life, stop the frantic chores, and enjoy the world around us.

I try to keep Saturday as my Sabbath as I'm usually preaching or working at church on Sunday. An ideal Saturday for me begins with a long prayer and meditation time, followed by a yoga class, followed by sitting in the sun completing a crossword puzzle, and then a nap, followed by dinner with good friends. Your ideal Sabbath may look completely different; it might be vigorous exercise or sitting and watching a game on television. The activities that refresh you are yours alone; what is important is a full, 24-hour break from your work routine and that at the end of it, you feel renewed and restored. It is a time for you and your loved ones just to be, not to try to get anything accomplished.

———— ☉ ————

Try it for a few weeks. Think about what a day devoted just to recharging and renewing would look like for you. Turn off your phone, email, iPad and other technology. Plan special foods to eat, or special rituals to share with those you love. Let others know that you are observing one day of rest each week, just like God intended. What can you plan for this week's Sabbath?

LOVE YOUR NEIGHBOR AS YOURSELF.

Leviticus 19:18

"Love your neighbor as yourself" first appears in the Bible in the book of Leviticus. It is part of a long list of instructions known as the "holiness code" that lays out the principles of a moral life. The full line is "You shall not take vengeance or bear a grudge against any of your people, but you shall love your neighbor as yourself. I am the Lord."

In the Gospels of Matthew (22:36–40), Mark (12:28–34) and Luke (10:27) a Pharisee asks Jesus, "Teacher, which commandment in the law is the greatest?" Reflecting this passage in Leviticus, he answers, "You shall love the Lord your God with all your heart, and with all your soul, and with all your mind. This is the greatest and first commandment. And a second is like it: you shall love your neighbor as yourself. On these two commandments hang all the law and the prophets."

Love your neighbor as yourself is one of the central Biblical themes. I love that it says "love" your neighbor—not *treat* your neighbor as yourself, but bring your whole heart and goodness to your neighbor. Scripture does not adequately address whom we are to consider our neighbor; surely it is not just the people who live in proximity to us. I like to think that since we are all created in God's image, we are called to understand *everyone* as our neighbor.

Almost every religion has a form of this, the Golden

Rule. The Dalai Lama has written, "Every religion emphasizes human improvement, love, respect for others, and sharing other people's suffering." Plato, who lived some 400 hundred years before the first century, writes in his *Republic*, "it has been shown that to injure anyone is never just anywhere." Islam, in the Hadith, teaches in gendered language, "None of you [truly] believes until he wishes for his brother what he wishes for himself."

There is a story told about the great Hebrew sage, Hillel, who lived about a hundred years before Jesus. A non-Jewish man challenged him by saying, "Convert me on the condition that you teach me the whole Torah while I stand on one foot." Hillel said to him, "That which is despicable to you, do not do to your fellow. This is the whole Torah, and the rest is commentary. Go and learn it."

I also like that this passage reminds us of how important it is to love ourselves. Several years ago I preached a sexuality sermon in Schenectady, New York. I talked about the Unitarian Universalist commitment to sexuality education, reproductive justice, and LGBT full inclusion.

A woman came up to me in the coffee hour. "I really disagreed with something you said," she told me. "I'm not surprised," I answered. "I know I talk about controversial things. Which part did you disagree with?" She said, "That part about love your neighbor as yourself and the dignity and worth of all people." I answered, "Oh, you mean like how does that extend to people like terrorists or Hitler?" She looked at me, puzzled. "No, I mean people right here. People I don't like very much, who sit on committees with me — they don't deserve my love or respect."

I thought to myself, the hardest part of loving your neighbor as yourself may be loving yourself first. I wondered if she loved herself and how she was tone deaf to the irony in her words.

Stop reading and take a few minutes to ponder, "Do I love myself? Do I really truly love, respect and honor the person I am? Am I living my life with the dignity in which I appreciate others? What is getting in the way of my loving myself, and how might I address those challenges?"

Others have suggested that the Golden Rule needs to be tweaked into a "Platinum Rule" that encourages, "Love others *as they want to be loved.*" The reality is that *you* may not want to be treated the way *I* want to be treated; you may need different things than I do. How subtle but how different that is.

"Love others as they want to be loved" calls us into profound relationships with others because first I have to take the time to find out about you, your culture, your background, your personality, your wants and your deepest desires. It requires me to be infinitely curious about what makes you tick. It calls me into communication with you, because I have to *ask you* to find out how you would like me to treat you. It removes *me* as the central reference in our relationship, but places *you* in the center of how I will behave towards you.

Do onto others are they would like you to do onto them. Treat others as they want to be treated. How could you start today?

THE WORD IS VERY NEAR TO YOU; IT IS IN YOUR MOUTH AND IN YOUR HEART FOR YOU TO OBSERVE.... I HAVE SET BEFORE YOU LIFE OR DEATH, BLESSINGS AND CURSES. CHOOSE LIFE SO THAT YOU AND YOUR DESCENDENTS MAY LIVE.

Deuteronomy 30:14, 19

This passage in Deuteronomy comes towards the end of Moses's life and time in the wilderness. Moses is speaking God's words to his followers, reminding them that their future deliverance is dependent on following God's laws. The early part of Deuteronomy 30 is almost threatening. The tribes are reminded that because people had deserted the covenant, that "in anger, in fury, in great wrath, (God) cast them into another land" (Deut. 29:28). This is not a warm, fuzzy God.

Indeed, we know today that this part of the Bible was probably written during the period of the monarchy (about 8 BCE) and addressed to the people in the Northern Kingdom. Although the history of that time is not completely known, what is clear is that the community is in crisis and the authors are seeking to describe a new, revitalized society. They are also seeking to re-engage the people into Jewish life.

It is perhaps not such a comforting overall passage

in that context, especially for those of us who resonate more to a revealed word rather than a legalistic one. But I like the words in lines 14 and 19 and see hope in their promise that we can choose rebirth and renewal.

Moses says the way to a good and just life is not in heaven, it's not beyond the seas, and it's not beyond our strength or our reach. No, it is very near to us—in our mouths and in our hearts for our own observance. It reminds us that we have everything we need; indeed, we have always had everything we need to find a way to be fulfilled and happy.

Victor Frankl, in *Man's Search for Meaning*, speaks of his time in the World War II concentration camps in this way:

> "The one thing you can't take away from me is the way I choose to respond to what you do to me. The last of one's freedoms is to choose one's attitude in any given circumstance."

Line 19 says to me that we make the choice to live well. Each day is full of choices between blessings and curses. For some of us, it is a stark choice. Do we continue drinking or do we start on the path to sobriety? Do we allow our depression to keep us in bed or do we get up and make the call to the doctor for help? Do we stand up to the spouse who has been abusing us or do we tiptoe around to avoid the explosion? And so on.

But most of us face the choice between blessing and curse on a much more mundane level every day. Are we short with our children or do we remember to tell them we love them? Do we take the time to bring a co-worker a cup of coffee and say thank you for a job well done, or do we snap at our colleagues in frustration? Do we swear at the driver ahead of us who is going too slowly or do we choose to have compassion for the difficulty they may be having that we are not privy to? Do we choose to bless or curse those who surround us?

I also experience something more transcendent in these words. "Choose life" is a reminder that life is a precious gift, and it can be wasted or fully savored. We all have times when we despair, when it seems hard to go on, hard to move forward. Deuteronomy 30:19 says "Choose life so that you…may live." Make the choice that is life enhancing, that will feed you, that will enrich you, rather than one that is life-deadening or harmful to yourself or others. If you need help, ask for it. Seek it. But choose to be life-affirming today.

WHERE YOU GO, I WILL GO; WHERE YOU LODGE, I WILL LODGE; YOUR PEOPLE SHALL BE MY PEOPLE, AND YOUR GOD MY GOD.

Ruth 1:16–17

You may have heard these words spoken at a wedding. In the book of Ruth, they are spoken by one woman to another, a daughter-in-law to her grieving mother-in-law, on a trip back to Naomi's hometown. Naomi has told Ruth it is time for her to return to her own family. Ruth responds with these words of love and commitment. She stays with Naomi, and they go on to have a new family together. The child Ruth bears is a "restorer...of life and nourisher of [Naomi's] old age" (Ruth 4:15). The child, Obed, "became the father of Jesse, the father of David" (Ruth 4:17), and an ancestor of Jesus (Matt. 1:5).

Ruth commits to Naomi fully. She pledges to go where she goes, live where she lives, and become part of her community and family. It is surely an unusual declaration from a daughter-in-law who in essence is promising to be a life partner. The passage reminds us we can fully join another in life.

It is also a story of full inclusion and acceptance of people who are different than us. Ruth is a Moabite; Naomi is from Judah. The country of Moab is an enemy of Judah; the people different and viewed as strange. Ruth offers to go with her mother-in-law, and

Naomi accepts her fully into her life. She becomes the "daughter-in-law who loves you, who is more to you than seven sons" (Ruth 4:15). Their love intensifies to a level beyond what a mother feels for her own children. As a mother, I can understand how deep that passage says their love was.

It also speaks of hope. King David and Jesus are the heirs of the decision made on this journey. Had Ruth turned back, like her sister-in-law Orpah (yes, Orpah; "Oprah" is a misspelling of this name), King David and Jesus would not have been born. Really. The entire narrative of the rest of the Bible would have had to be different.

It is in our decisions and actions today that the future unfolds. Our commitments to other people matter. By welcoming people into our lives, no matter how different, we can change the world. Ruth and Naomi did. So can you.

You show me the path of life. In your presence there is fullness of joy; in your right hand are pleasures forevermore.

Psalm 16:11

Psalm 16 is a song of joy and awe. The psalmist blesses God, reminds the listener that the "Lord (is) always before me" (Ps. 16:8) and talks about the heart being glad and the soul rejoicing. God in this psalm promises joy and pleasure always.

How far from a world of sinners this psalm is. Instead, it is a reminder to delight in the world—and the life—we have been given. Contemporary poet Mary Oliver in her poem "Look and See" talks about the beauty of the physical world in this way: "Oh Lord, how shining and festive is your gift to us, if we only look, and see."

This psalm reminds us to look for daily pleasures. Think for a moment: what pleasures await you today? For me, today, it will involve a walk on a beautiful September day during lunch time, a massage appointment at the end of the day, a promised phone call with one of my best friends. Tomorrow I will have other pleasures, if I choose to create them.

The psalm also reminds me that my belief in a beneficent God, a goodness in the Universe that I can trust, can help me relax into today. If I can trust in that goodness, I can be less stressed, less anxious about tomorrow.

Each night before bed, I try to remember to say this prayer, that I understand comes from the Unity tradition.

> "The Light of God surrounds me;
> The Love of God enfolds me;
> The Power of God protects me;
> The Presence of God watches over me....
> Wherever I am, God is...
> And all is well."

It comforts me, just as the ancient psalms comforted people, and reminds me that I am never alone. If you are not a theist, it works as a poem with "love" substituting for God language:

> "The Light of Love surrounds me;
> Love enfolds me;
> The Power of Love protects me;
> Love watches over me....
> Wherever I am, Love is...
> And all is well."

Try it tonight and see.

THE LORD IS MY SHEPHERD, I SHALL NOT WANT. GOD MAKES ME LIE DOWN IN GREEN PASTURES; GOD LEADS ME BESIDES STILL WATERS; GOD RESTORES MY SOUL. GOD LEADS ME IN RIGHT PATHS FOR GOD'S NAME'S SAKE.

Psalm 23:1–3

The 23rd Psalm is probably the most familiar of all the psalms. It is the first psalm I wanted to memorize, and it is the one people most often request of me to read or recite when I visit hospital patients or serve at funerals.

The image of God as shepherd is deeply comforting, even in 21st-century America when many of us have never actually seen a shepherd tending a flock except in paintings or movies. Yet we understand and resonate to the image of a beneficent presence being with us, watching over us, keeping us safe, fed, and on the path of goodness, of holiness. Our hearts yearn for not wanting anything except to be satisfied by the lives we do have. I like this image of God being with us—removed, yet gently guiding and providing for us always.

Many years ago I spent time on a goat farm in southern France, and I served as a goatherd for a few days. The rolling hills stretched beyond where one could see; the hills were lit by the warmth of the sun. After walking the goats from their pens to the hill, we were told that our task was simply to watch and make sure none of the goats wandered off alone. At the end of the day, our job was to round them up and lead them back to the village. The goats fanned over the hills, and from a distance, we kept a sleepy eye on them so that none strayed too far. Everything the goats needed for the day was provided by those grassy hills and the stream that meandered through them. There was nothing else they needed; they did not want.

They didn't need our help to eat, drink, sleep, or do whatever other goat-like things they did during the day. Their days were framed by the essence of "goat", and all they needed was periodic gentle guidance. Our purpose there was only to assure their safety and their return home. We sat quietly, observing, enjoying the sun, letting the day pass, needing only a few times to encourage a wayward goat to return closer to the others. Relationship restored, we could go back to our own quiet meditation.

Perhaps we need to spend more days like shepherds. Rather than trying to direct our children, our employees, our partners—indeed the world—with our desires and needs for them, we might step back and view ourselves as guides. Our main job is to give others the space to be the essence of who they are and to encourage them in relationship to others. I'm not always so good at this, so I keep a sticky note on my office monitor to remind me to "bless more, control less."

———— ✑ ————

Just for today, relax and believe that God is your shepherd and that you shall not want. Remind yourself that all that you need spiritually is being provided for you today. Remember that you are enough, just the way you are. Seek to be the shepherd for others—not controlling, not directing, but letting them be exactly who they are. Feel your soul restored.

EVEN THOUGH I WALK THROUGH THE DARKEST VALLEY, I FEAR NO EVIL; FOR YOU ARE WITH ME.... SURELY GOODNESS AND MERCY SHALL FOLLOW ME ALL THE DAYS OF MY LIFE, AND I SHALL DWELL IN THE HOUSE OF THE LORD MY WHOLE LIFE LONG.

Psalm 23:4, 6

Death is inevitable. Every one of us, every person we love, every person we admire, every person we dislike, all will die. As much as we all want to live as if that weren't true, we are indeed walking in the shadow of death.

It might seem strange to you that I've included this reminder in a book about the "good news" of the Bible. Surely we have all known the pain of the death of someone we love and the illnesses that take people away too soon. You may have struggled with the sure knowledge that one day you too will die. I know I have.

But this second passage from the 23rd Psalm, while acknowledging universal mortality, contains promises for *this* life. Goodness and mercy will be with us all of our lives, the psalmist wrote. And then he or she emphasized, not even half a verse later, that we will dwell in this wonderful creation, "our whole life long." We need not fear, for we have the opportunity to live and create our lives *now*.

My colleague Rev. Forrest Church, who died too early at the age of 61, wrote:

> "Religion is our human response to the dual reality of being alive and having to die. Knowing that we must die, we question what life means. The answers we arrive at may not be religious answers, but the questions death forces us to ask are, at heart, religious questions. Where did I come from? Who am I? Where am I going? What is life's purpose? What does it all signify?"

When I was younger, I hated the thought of dying prematurely, especially before my children were grown and launched. In middle age, I am much more concerned about future suffering and living past my usefulness. Time spent with congregants and family members with end stage diseases or Alzheimer's in nursing homes has convinced me to be sure that I have a living will, a health care proxy, and that I have been clear about my wishes for no heroic measures or feeding tubes to prolong my life. (I highly recommend the 12-page booklet by Five Wishes, agingwithdignity. org/five-wishes.php, for you and your loved ones to think through your final wishes.) I am clear and have made my intentions known to my family that I do not want to spend my last days in pain or being kept alive by artificial means.

But more, this passage calls me to understand in Forrest's beautifully written words, "Death is not life's goal, only life's terminus. The goal is to live in such a way that our lives will prove worth dying for."

To live so that our lives will prove worth dying for. We all have the ability to create a life that does just that. Stop and ask yourself, if you were to die tomorrow, would those you love say that you loved your life and lived it well? Could you say it?

And if not, what do you need to begin to change? The 23rd Psalm reminds us that the gift is being alive, that we can rest with the assurance that goodness and mercy will characterize our lives.

Because we can make it so. Yes, life, as Buddhism teaches us, is suffering. But how we react to that suffering is in our individual control. We can be defeated or we can look for what we can learn in difficult situations. We can resist or we can pray and hope. We can isolate or we can reach out. We can protect ourselves or we can love again. May we love again.

WEEPING MAY LINGER FOR THE NIGHT, BUT JOY COMES WITH THE MORNING.

Psalm 30:5

There are times in everyone's life when our sorrow is so deep that it seems like we will never be happy again. A loved one has died, a child or a lover is seriously ill, a dear friend moves away, a child leaves home, someone tells us that they no longer want to be in a relationship with us. We may actually feel sensations of grief, deep in our chest, that our heart is breaking. At the beginning we may be wracked, sobbing great tears, crying from a place so deep inside us that just moments prior we didn't even know existed. A little later, little reminders of that person cause us to break into tears at unexpected moments.

You may be feeling that way now. Surely most of us have had this experience by our mid- to late twenties, some of us much earlier. When we love, truly love, other people—children, friends, family members, partners—when they leave us, whether through moving or death or just moving on, our hearts break.

Yet, Psalm 30 teaches that God can turn "mourning into dancing" (Ps. 30:11) and that "joy comes with the morning" (Ps. 30:5). This is no hollow platitude, a "you'll get over it" as too many parents counsel their teens getting over first love. It is instead God's promise. Joy will return.

Why? The passage reminds us that our sorrow is so deep precisely because we have allowed ourselves the vulnerability, the intimacy of truly loving another. We would not hurt so much if we hadn't loved so much. And the experience of that lost love affirms that we have the capacity to love again.

If you are feeling deep sorrow now, be with it. Don't wish it away, don't hurry your grief. Cry, talk about it, allow yourself to be overwhelmed. Look at photos, collect your memories. Sit with your loss.

If you are a friend of someone who is mourning, just be with him or her. You don't have to "do" anything. Sit together. Listen. Be present. You only need to say, "I'm sorry" and mean it.

Remind yourself that happiness can and will return. Some of us may need medical or psychological help to get through these periods; all of us will need time.

Even in your grief, try to do one little thing that pleases you today. Breathe in a flower. Drink a good cup of coffee. Stretch your body. Go for a walk. Allow yourself a few moments to remember that life is good. Joy will come again.

MY HEART IS STEADFAST, O GOD, MY HEART IS STEADFAST; I WILL SING AND MAKE MELODY. AWAKE MY SOUL! AWAKE, O HARP AND LYRE! I WILL AWAKE THE DAWN.

Psalm 108:1–2

"My heart is steadfast." Steadfast is not a word we use much today. It means unwavering. Resolute. Committed. Dedicated. Unswerving. It speaks to me of commitment but also of calmness. Of knowing who I am, what I have to do, and feeling peace in the midst of it.

I have a card on my desk by an unknown author that reads, "Peace. It does not mean to be in a place where there is no noise, trouble or hard work. It means to be in the midst of those things and still be calm in your heart."

When we feel that way—about ourselves, or a relationship, or a career, or God—we feel truly engaged in our lives and more alive. We feel centered in ourselves. We may feel a sense of grace, that all is right with the world.

Some writers talk about "flow"—those moments in which we somehow transcend our daily consciousness or the busy chatter of our minds and become completely engaged in what we are doing. I know that feeling at times when I am teaching, praying aloud with someone, preaching, and when I am writing. I forget who I am for just those moments, become completely present and at one with what I am doing. I wonder what activities make you feel that way.

In those moments, we are indeed making music. Our souls feel more awake. We may not actually hear celestial harps and lyres like in 1940s black-and-white movies, but we do feel a sense of oneness. This passage promises that all of us have the potential to wake up our souls.

Many ancient and modern day philosophies and practices encourage being mindful in the moment. Buddhism asks its practitioners to stay present and not become attached to the outcome. Thousands of years later, Ram Dass popularized, "be here now." The EST program of the 1970s and its successor The Landmark Forum taught people that "getting it" meant paying attention to the present moment. Dr. Jon Kabat-Zinn created mindfulness meditation as a response to stress, anxiety and daily pressures but also to help people learn to stay present in the current moment.

I love the last part of verse two: "I will awake the dawn." When we are fully present and fully engaged, we bring our own sun, our own light to the earth. People around us can't help but feel our new beginning, the power of our being fully alive and present. We too can awake the dawn.

How might we create more of these moments? Meditation may be one way. Finding what we love to do and making sure we have time to do it is another. It might be singing in a chorus, creating a craft, volunteering for others, playing a sport, developing a yoga practice. Perhaps for you it is daily prayer or reading. Or maybe it is in encounters with others or with God.

The passage ends with the reminder that the divine

is with us at these times: "For your steadfast love is higher than the heavens, and your faithfulness reaches to the clouds" (Ps. 108:4). God wants us to sing, make melodies, and awake the dawn with our aliveness.

What can you awaken within yourself today? What can you bring awake in the world?

I PRAISE YOU, FOR I AM FEARFULLY AND WONDERFULLY MADE. WONDERFUL ARE YOUR WORKS; THAT I KNOW VERY WELL.

Psalm 139:14

The human body is a wondrous gift. Take a minute to think about how amazing your body is. You breathe as you need to, your heart beats without your intervention, your digestive system breaks down food into the nutrients you need, your blood courses through your veins, bringing oxygen to your cells, and so on—and we don't have to direct or manage any of those autonomic systems.

The psalmist knew little about how the systems of the body actually worked or about how fetuses develop in "my mother's womb" (Ps. 139–13). But even thousands of years later, with all our intricate understanding of biology, we too can experience the awe of the gift of our bodies, including how we develop prenatally to birth to childhood to adolescence through all the stages of adulthood.

As the psalmist writes, we are fearfully and wonderfully made. "Fearfully" is used here to mean awe inspiring, but also perhaps it is the psalmist's recognition that our bodies are fragile systems and that like any precious gift, we must honor and take care of it.

How easy it is to take our bodies for granted. Except when we are sick or beset with a chronic condition, we pay little attention to being "wonderfully made." We become aware of our skeletal system only when we have back or knee pain; we don't think about our immune systems except when we get a cold or flu; we become aware of the miracle of healthy cells after the cancer diagnosis. Too many of us threaten our health by ignoring our needs for good nutrition, exercise, rest, and stress reduction.

And too many of us feel badly about our bodies because they don't fit the media-driven models of attractiveness. We believe ourselves to be too fat, too thin, too curly-haired, too old, too wrinkled, too grey; few of us in America like our bodies just the way they are. But regardless of how we compare to the toned, buff, sexy, young, ultrathin celebrity visions, we must not forget that all of our bodies are miraculous.

How we take care of the precious gift of our bodies is a way to praise God. Self-care can be re-imagined as a spiritual practice. When I am taking care of and enjoying my body—feeding it healthy food, exercising regularly, meditating, enjoying sexual pleasures with my husband—I am honoring its gifts.

Parker Palmer, writing about his own journey, said:

"Self-care is never a selfish act—it is simply good stewardship of the only gift I have, the gift I was put on earth to offer to others. Anytime we can listen to true self and give it the care it requires, we do so not only for ourselves but for the many others whose lives we touch."

Take some moments to think about how miraculous it is that you can sit here reading, thinking, breathing, and feeling. Perhaps echoing Psalm 139, the poet e.e. cummings wrote:

> "how should tasting touching hearing
> seeing/ breathing any—lifted from the no/
> of all nothing—human merely being/doubt
> unimaginable You?"

Thank your body today—just the way it is. Celebrate it. Take care of it. Offer praise for it. You are wondrously made.

LET YOUR FOUNTAIN BE BLESSED, AND REJOICE IN THE WIFE OF YOUR YOUTH, A LOVELY DEER, A GRACEFUL DOE. MAY HER BREASTS SATISFY YOU AT ALL TIMES; MAY YOU BE INTOXICATED ALWAYS BY HER LOVE.

Proverbs 5:18–19

Scripture recognizes, as today's sexologists do, that sexuality is a lifelong part of life. This proverb expresses the hope for lifelong love and eroticism in a long-term relationship.

Earlier in the Bible, the special role of sexuality in the first year of a sexual relationship is underscored in Deuteronomy: "When a man is newly married, he shall not go out with the army or be charged with any related duty. He shall be free at home one year, to be happy with the wife whom he has married" (Deut. 24:5). I once read a passage from Martin Luther in 15th century in which he wrote about this passage: It is "as though Moses wanted to say, 'The joy will last for a year; after that we shall see.'" Today's sexual scientists have research that backs up what most people know and this Deuteronomy verse underscores: Sexual frequency is never higher than in the first year of a sexual relationship.

How joyous that the book of Proverbs includes these

lines that sexual relationships continue throughout life. We know that even among the most elderly, people can continue to enjoy eroticism with a partner or with themselves. As we live longer, people are falling in love again in their eighties and nineties and forming new relationships. And what is sweeter than celebrating a good, vibrant fifty- or sixty-year-old partnership or marriage?

In 2011, when marriage equality became a reality in New York State, I had the privilege of performing a wedding for two 87-year-old men who had been together for 57 years. In their vows, one said to the other, "I have woken up every day in love with you." Everyone there had tears in their eyes.

This passage intimates what we also know if we have been in long-term sexual relationships: that desire often does fade and sexual contact often recedes. I loved reading this anonymous comment left on a blog post that was shared with me by a friend; it too echoes these words in Proverbs:

> "The sexiest body is the body that belongs to the woman I love; be it too skinny or too round by the standard of the day. As a man who has been with the same woman for 40 years, I will tell you that I love every curve and every place where there once was a curve because it is the body that gave me children, missed me being next to her when I traveled and held me tight when I failed."

This passage is another recognition that the Bible teaches a view of sexuality that is positive and life affirming. Far from associating sexual relationships with sin, the Bible teaches us that sexual relationships are sacred and to be enjoyed. How can you celebrate that today?

A GENERATION GOES, AND A GENERATION COMES, BUT THE EARTH REMAINS FOREVER. THE SUN RISES AND THE SUN GOES DOWN, AND HURRIES TO THE PLACE WHERE IT RISES .... THE PEOPLE OF LONG AGO ARE NOT REMEMBERED, NOR WILL THERE BE ANY REMEMBRANCE OF PEOPLE YET TO COME.

Ecclesiastes 1:4–5, 11

It is so easy to forget, in both the struggles and joys and the everydayness of our lives, that we are alive for such a brief moment in time. The writer of the book of Ecclesiastes is known as Qoheleth, the teacher or the prophet. I picture Qoheleth as a middle-aged man or woman, facing the certainty of death to come, wondering how to live the best life possible, and knowing that his life will come to an end.

I get that. I'm 58 as I write this, and acutely aware, in a new way, that my life will not go on forever. I am aware that I am getting older, and that sometime in the next fifteen, twenty, thirty years, I will no longer have the same energy, health, and stamina that I do now. That despite all of my efforts at resisting aging, if I am lucky, I will one day be old. And that I will one day die.

I find these words in the opening chapter of Ecclesiastes oddly comforting and yes, good news. The earth will go on without me. The sun will rise and the sun will set, and within a few generations, no one will remember me. With very few exceptions, most of us will be forgotten or live on only as very imprecise memories of generations to come.

I love watching sunrises and sunsets. Partly, because of their immense beauty as the colors fan out across the sky. But also because they remind me in a very real way how insignificant I really am. The universe operates independently of me, of you. The sunrise and the sunset remind me that I am not in control, and that life will go on after me, just as it did before me.

I was on a train recently at dawn, facing an open window. The sun began to rise, first as a glimmer of light, and then electrifying the sky with the most beautiful orange and pinks and yellows. I forgot I was on a train: my heart sang with the colors and the returning light. I was entranced by the beauty, and then the thought arose in my mind, "This will not always be so. Pay attention." I felt my heart crack open; I was alive. It was beautiful. My moments like this are limited. I will not always be. The sun will rise and set long after I am. But for now, I am. And I watched the sun paint the sky for another day.

What if we woke up each day and said "Thank you"? What if we woke up each day, ready to pay attention to all of the good things that the universe offers? Qoheleth says to pay attention now. Enjoy what the world offers. Take pleasure in this day; it will not always be so.

For everything there is a season, and a time for every matter under heaven.

Ecclesiastes 3:1

Pete Seeger, the folk singer, used the words from Ecclesiastes 3 in his song, "Turn, Turn, Turn" in 1959. For those of us of a certain age, it's hard to read this passage without hearing Pete Seeger or the Byrds or maybe our friends at summer camp singing these lyrics.

I am especially fond of the poem that contains this verse in the third chapter of Ecclesiastes, and I have used it for the titles of a series of publications on sexuality issues in congregations. *A Time to Build* is about creating a sexually healthy and responsible faith community. *A Time to Seek* is a guide on sexual and gender diversity. *A Time to Speak* addresses sexuality education in the faith community. *A Time to be Born* offers help to those struggling with infertility. *A Time to Heal* is about preventing child sexual abuse. I expect one day to write a book, *A Time to Embrace*, about sexuality and faith.

This poem contrasts times of difficulty with times of joy—a time to break down with a time to build up, a time to weep with a time to laugh, a time to love with a time to hate, a time for war with a time for peace. Each of the lines ends with the positive, emphasizing the hope for what is good and pleasant in life.

The passage reminds me that each of our lives has struggles and joyful times. Like the passage from Psalm

30 on page 30, we are consoled by remembering that difficult times are often balanced by coming periods of joy. Goethe wrote similarly in words that have consoled me during my own challenges, "Sometimes our fate resembles a fruit tree in winter. Who would think that those branches would turn green again and blossom, but we hope it, we know it." We can rely on it, just as we can rely on spring following winter. For everything there is a season.

Indeed, after difficult times in my life, I have often realized that I have learned something new about myself or the world that I wouldn't have understood without having gone through the pain. As a chaplain in the oncology ward of my local hospital, I often heard people saying that cancer was a gift to them, teaching them not to take time or other people for granted. My time working with them was a reminder to be grateful without having to experience cancer, grateful that I would go home healthy at night to a loving partner and my children when my patients could not.

In "a time for every matter under heaven" I also hear a soft voice calling us to develop a sense of patience, calm and satisfaction in our lives. There is time enough to enjoy the life we have been given. We have time to laugh, dance, embrace, speak and love.

Can you take that sense of happiness and enjoyment into today? Remind yourself that today is the only day you know for certain you will have. Tell the people you love that you love them. Think about how you can have some time today with laughter...movement...physical touch...and intentionally bring that into your day. Take time for every matter under heaven.

I KNOW THAT THERE IS NOTHING BETTER FOR THEM THAN TO BE HAPPY AND ENJOY THEMSELVES AS LONG AS THEY LIVE; MOREOVER, IT IS GOD'S GIFT THAT ALL SHOULD EAT AND DRINK AND TAKE PLEASURE IN ALL THEIR TOIL.

Ecclesiastes 3:12–13

When I told my friend Rabbi Dennis Sasso that I was working on a book of meditations to demonstrate that the Bible wants us to enjoy life, he responded, "Oh, you must be writing about the book of Ecclesiastes." The encouragement that people should eat, drink, enjoy our relationships, and enjoy our work appears seven times in the book of Ecclesiastes.

As indicated in the passage on page 41, the author of Ecclesiastes is coming to grips with the certainty of death and the fleeting nature of life. Throughout the book, Qohelet counsels that people should enjoy their lives and be happy. He is not counseling people to eat or drink excessively, but rather to acknowledge that there are pleasures available to all.

I like that Qohelet encourages people to find "pleasure in their toil." I resonate with the saying, "if you love your job, you'll never work a day in your life." I am fortunate that I love my work in the world, and truly find pleasure in being a minister and a sexuality educator, offering counseling, training professionals, and writing books and articles. I am on-my-knees grateful for all of the opportunities my vocation has brought in my life.

And I know that's unusual. Too many people struggle in jobs that don't give them pleasure or satisfaction. Many people have to work at tasks or in environments that don't offer fulfilling and enjoyable activities. Some people get caught up in making a certain level of salary and other people feel lucky in today's economy to have paid employment at all.

Loving what you do means first finding out what you love to do. I have told my own children that I don't care what career they prepare for but I do hope that they will discover what they are passionate about and devote themselves to creating employment opportunities that involve that passion. This passage reminds us that one of God's gifts to us is the chance to find meaningful work. Rev. Dr. Frederick Buechner, a writer and Presbyterian minister, wrote that finding one's vocation is understanding "where the world's greatest need meets your greatest joy."

Unlike the religious views that all humans are sinners or destined to live a life of suffering, this passage also tells us that God wants humans to be happy and "enjoy themselves as long as they live." It is not that we won't struggle or be faced with challenges, but Qoheleth hopes that we will bring an optimistic attitude towards our lives and that we will seek what makes us happy. There is a line in the Talmud that says, "In the world to come each of us will be called to account for all the good things God put on earth which we refused to enjoy." Nature, food, friendships and sexual pleasure are part of those "good things."

We now know that there is a genetic component to happiness; some of us naturally find happiness easier than others. But research also tells us that happiness in life is based more on our daily choices and actions than our genetics. People who are happier exercise; spend time in nature; do good deeds and serve others; take the time for daily reflection through journaling or meditating; have a strong support network including family and friends; belong to a religious community; and express gratitude each day.

Choose to be happy. Cultivate actions and activities that support happiness. Just for today, make a commitment to bring your most positive attitude into the world. Remember that being happy is one way to honor God's gift to us.

OH, MAY YOUR BREASTS BE LIKE CLUSTERS OF THE VINE, AND THE SCENT OF YOUR BREATH LIKE APPLES, AND YOUR KISSES LIKE THE BEST WINE THAT GOES DOWN SMOOTHLY, GLIDING OVER LIPS AND TEETH.

Song of Solomon 7:8–9

When I ask audiences what the core messages are about sex in the Bible, someone usually says "Don't have it", and the rest of the audience laughs. And then I ask, "Is there *any* reason the Bible says to have sex?" and people shout out, "Procreation."

Sometimes I read them the above passage from the book called the Song of Solomon, also known as the Song of Songs or the Canticles. Many who don't know the Bible well are surprised that the Bible contains such an erotic passage. They are even more surprised when I read them other passages with even more sexually explicit images that leave no doubt that this is seduction:

"How fair and pleasant you are
O loved one, delectable maiden!
You are stately as a palm tree
and your breasts are like its clusters.

I say I will climb the palm tree
and lay hold of its branches."

Song 7:6–8

Or this even more explicit one about sexual desire
and arousal:

"My beloved thrust his hand into the opening,
and my inmost being yearned for him.
I arose to open to my beloved,
and my hand dripped with myrrh,
my fingers with liquid myrrh."

Song 5:4–5

The Song describes an erotic relationship between
an unmarried man and woman who are matched in
their sexual desire. In the *Harper's Bible Commentary*,
theologian Marcia Falk writes about the Song of Songs,
"Women speak as assertively as men, initiating action at
least as often; men are free to be as gentle, as vulnerable,
even as coy as women. Men and women similarly praise
each other for their sensuality and their beauty, and
identical phrases are sometimes used to describe lovers
of both genders." The Song does not talk about sex
in the context of marriage or procreation; the woman
in the Song is never "called a wife, nor is she required
to bear children. In fact, to the issue of marriage and
procreation, the Song does not speak," writes Falk.

I would have liked to have been present as the
proverbial fly on the wall when those who decided what
would be included in the canon, the official books and
order of the Bible, were debating whether to include

the Song. I can only imagine that there were some who thought that this erotic love poem did not belong in this most holy Book. But they *did* decide to include it, in all its erotic imagery and mutuality.

How wonderful that the Bible celebrates the gift of sexuality. Far from labeling sexuality or sexual relationships as sinful, these passages and others (see pages 7, 38, and 50) underscore that our sexuality is a sacred and life-fulfilling gift, and integral to our spirituality.

Interestingly, after Genesis and Psalms, the Song was the most frequently expounded book of the Old Testament in the Middle Ages. Some early theologians warned against the text, writing that the Song should not be read by anyone under 30, and that people would be harmed by its reading. But you weren't harmed, right?

Take some time to think about what it means to you that there is a book in the Bible that celebrates erotic attraction, desire and arousal. If you grew up in a religious tradition that taught that your desires were sinful or needed to be confessed, be open to how this learning might change you. Think about what it would mean to teach young people today that their sexuality was sacred and therefore should never be abused or exploited. If you have a sexual partner, think about how you might bring an attitude of reverence and sacredness to your next sexual encounter. Or just smile, knowing that the Bible teaches that sexuality is a blessed part of life.

FOR YOU SHALL GO OUT WITH JOY, AND BE LED BACK IN PEACE; THE MOUNTAINS AND THE HILLS BEFORE YOU SHALL BURST INTO SONG, AND ALL THE TREES OF THE FIELD SHALL CLAP THEIR HANDS.

Isaiah 55:12

This passage comes at the end of the second book of Isaiah. Second Isaiah is a long series of fiery speeches on how the exiled people can become a unified Israel once again. God has been angry with the people of Israel, but has now renewed the covenant out of the favors promised to David (Isa. 55:3–5).

In the translation called *The Jerusalem Bible,* these verses are labeled "The Conclusion of the Book on Consolation." We know what it is to need to be consoled. Our heart has been broken; our days have been hard; the children have been needy; the discomfort from our physical or mental health issues seems to be at a breaking point. We seek to know that life will be better again.

And the prophet Isaiah, at the height of the Babylonian exile, says just that—you will leave with joy and be led back in peace.

Sometimes we need to retreat, to pull back from our everyday lives, in order to refresh and revitalize. If we are fortunate, perhaps we can go on a vacation to a beautiful place, such as mountains, hills and fields or a river or lake. Or perhaps what we can afford is a day in a city park or garden. Perhaps we can set aside a day to sit by ourselves in the woods or on the edge of the ocean.

Recent studies have shown just how important vacation is to our well being, and that even short breaks can be helpful. In fact, studies show that a three- or four-day break may be as reinvigorating as several weeks, and that it is often the planning of time off that gives the greatest joy. And yet many people are anxious and worried during their first days of time off. It's hard to turn off their everyday stresses, and surely as someone who travels for work nearly weekly, I know the hassles of airports and connections. This passage from Isaiah says to me, "Leave with a joyful heart" and trust — trust that you will be safe and the people you leave behind will be safe as well.

I also love the image of the world being happy that I'm taking a break. The mountains, hills and fields are joyful; the trees are clapping. What a glorious sight that would be.

Like many people, I find nature a great balm. After I've walked in the woods, or seen a beautiful vista, or climbed a mountain, I often feel a sense of inner calm and peace. Nature can indeed be nurture, reminding us that this beautiful world was created to sustain us. If we listen to the metaphors of Genesis, God formed the light, the land, the sky and the waters before God formed people. We are cradled by the natural world, and in this passage, the natural world is said to be delighted by us.

Like so many people today, I work long hours, and because of technology, my working world and my personal world often blend into each other. I have sometimes allowed the hours of work I put in to lead me to a place of feeling burned out, overwhelmed, even physically ill.

I've learned that I need deep rest and renewal—and to be reset. This passage reminds me to leave it all behind sometimes. We do not serve God by burning ourselves out; indeed, we cannot serve God if we are. We must take the time to leave and trust that joy and safety will return. We can allow the mountains, hills and trees to console us and refill our souls. And then we can return again to our work with joy.

I WILL GIVE THEM AN EVERLASTING NAME.

Isaiah 56:5

You may remember the theme song from the television sitcom "Cheers" that ended, "where everybody knows your name." A recurring motif in the show was when one of the patrons at the bar entered and everyone together shouted, "Norm!"

Being known by your name is important. This passage from Isaiah says that the eunuchs, despised for their difference, would be given an "everlasting name." The Holocaust museum in Jerusalem derives its name from this passage, "Yad Vashem." Those murdered in the Holocaust have their names recorded there.

Think about how important your name is to you. What stories do you know about how your parents or guardians picked the name to give you? What is its history in your family? Did you like your name growing up? Do you like it now? Did you ever wish you were named something else?

Our names are important. People using our names are important.

Let me introduce you to what I call "name ministry." Every day there are people who perform services for us who often go without names. The person who bags your groceries. The woman at the dry cleaner. The man at the coffee place drive-thru. The postal worker. The TSA screener. And so on.

Some of these people wear name tags. But hardly anyone uses their names. They perform their daily work tasks, again and again, and for the most part, the people they serve accept their service, maybe say thank you, but fail to acknowledge them and their humanity. And they don't know your name either, even though you come in every day or every week, and maybe they even know that you are the "medium decaf, skim" without asking.

I believe that this passage in Isaiah calls us to use each other's names. To know each other's names. Name ministry means asking the name of every person with whom you come in contact and then using it. It means introducing yourself.

And it changes everything. When I walk into the Commuter Coffee takeout counter in the morning, I say, "Hi, Fred, how is your day going?" He says, "Good morning, Rev. Debra. What can I get you?" It's a different experience than just grunting my order and waiting impatiently.

When I handed my government-issued ID to a TSA agent recently, I said, "Good morning, Officer Gerald. I hope you are having a good day." She looked up in surprise, and then smiled. She then not only did whatever she does with my license, but she said, "Rev. Haffner, I hope you have a good flight." We will never see each other again, but we both felt a little better about ourselves, about the world.

It doesn't take but a moment, but it makes a difference. Find out someone's name today. Smile and use it. Pay attention to the person's response to you using their name. Pay attention to how it made you feel. It may not be an everlasting name, but it makes a difference.

THE LORD WILL GUIDE YOU CONTINUALLY, AND SATISFY YOUR NEEDS IN PARCHED PLACES, AND MAKE YOUR BONES STRONG; AND YOU SHALL BE LIKE A WATERED GARDEN, LIKE A SPRING OF WATER, WHOSE WATERS NEVER FAIL.

Isaiah 58:11

The image of God as shepherd or guide continues in this passage. But it takes the metaphor a step further for the people in Isaiah's time who were living in the desert where there were regular droughts and water could not be counted on. In this passage, Isaiah tells the people that they shall be like a beautiful garden, with blossoming flowers, running streams, and fountains, and that their needs will be satisfied.

I've recently been to a part of Kenya where the land is parched and the trees are bare. It is less than a few hundred miles from the Sudan border, where the drought has killed tens of thousands of people. And yet we would occasionally pass well watered farms where crops were growing and bougainvilleas were flourishing. I could see the promise of this passage in my mind as we drove by these farms.

Many of us have experienced droughts in our communities and the anxious wait for rain. I think of a visit a few years ago to a friend in Atlanta, which was experiencing a drought. My friend had committed to showering only once a week, and there were signs in her bathrooms not to flush the toilets often. The crisis of water around the world is extreme in many places, and as I write this, droughts are plaguing such diverse parts of the world as Canada, Mozambique and Argentina.

But I think we also all know what it is metaphorically to find ourselves in a drought. Maybe we are writers who can't call forth words. Maybe we are artists who are missing inspiration, craftspeople without new ideas. Maybe we have recently broken up with a partner and feel we won't love again. Maybe our lives feel parched and arid, and we believe that newness and refreshment are out of our grasp. You can surely think of such a time in your own life.

What promise there is in this passage. Just as God did not desert the Jews in the wilderness, God will not desert the people in exile — or us either. We need not fear the drought times of our lives, because ultimately the garden will flourish. If we have faith, we cannot fail. The God in this passage wants us to flourish and thrive, and promises to be with us always. We too can triumph over periods of doubt and dryness; in the beneficence of the divine, we can find our own well-fed gardens.

FOR SURELY I KNOW THE PLANS I HAVE FOR YOU, SAYS THE LORD, PLANS FOR YOUR WELFARE AND NOT FOR HARM, TO GIVE YOU A FUTURE WITH HOPE.

Jeremiah 29:11

For the most part, the series of the Biblical books known as the Prophets present a bleak and often intimidating picture. The book of Jeremiah recounts when the King of Babylon destroyed Jerusalem in 586 B.C.E., burned the Temple, executed the Jewish leaders, and exiled many of the survivors to Babylonia. Other Jews fled to Egypt. This period is referred to as the beginning of the Diaspora, and is perhaps most familiar to us from the words of the hymn based on Psalm 137:1: "By the rivers of Babylon—there we sat down and there we wept when we remembered Zion."

But even the bleakest of the Prophets held out for the promise of better days to come. Jeremiah predicts that the exile would last 70 years, but that there would be a return and that the Jewish people would thrive once again. One can imagine the Jews of the Middle Ages through the Holocaust remembering this promise from God in their darkest days.

The Prophets present a historical picture but can also speak to us metaphorically. Just as we have known the wilderness, we have known what it is to be in exile. Like me, I am sure there have been times you have felt that you were all alone, separated literally or figuratively from what had been familiar, from the life you had previously known. We all know what it is to despair and not to know what will come next.

And it is in those moments that our faith really matters. If we are theists, we can believe that God ultimately has plans for us for a better tomorrow, a "future with hope." The God in this passage is a benevolent God who wants the best for us. If we don't believe in God (or even if we do), we can still have faith in ourselves. We can remind ourselves that we have the resiliency to come through dark times, and we can reach out for help and support. We have emerged from exile before; we can do it again.

We may not see the answers or the hope in the dark moments, but we can believe that answers will emerge. I love this quote from German poet Rainier Maria Rilke, "Be patient toward all that is unsolved in your heart and try to love the questions themselves, like locked rooms and like books that are now written in a very foreign tongue. Do not now seek the answers, which cannot be given you because you would not be able to live them. And the point is, to live everything. Live the questions now. Perhaps you will then gradually, without noticing it, live along some distant day into the answer."

For today, have faith. Be patient. Let the answers emerge. Trust in your future with hope.

WHAT DOES THE LORD REQUIRE OF YOU BUT TO DO JUSTICE, AND TO LOVE KINDNESS, AND WALK TO HUMBLY WITH YOUR GOD.

Micah 6:8

The gods of the ancient world were often wrathful, willful, and capricious. In other words, they were very hard to please. At times, the God of the Hebrew Bible appears that way as well, destroying cities, banishing people, refusing to respond to prayers and petitions.

But in this passage from the book of Micah, God is much gentler, far less demanding. The passage before these more famous words says unlike those other gods who want people to give sacrifice and burnt offerings, our God only wants you to be the best person you can be and to live a righteous life.

Many of us grew up with demanding parents. Some of us grew up feeling that we were never able to do enough to please those parents. That's exhausting. No matter how hard we tried, we wouldn't be good enough. The Bs on the report card should have been all As. The junior team should have been varsity. The homemade card should have been store bought. Some people become perfectionists with these kinds of parents, always striving to achieve more. Other people become withdrawn or have shaky self-images, believing they will never match up to expectations.

Some people carry the "I'm not good enough" or "my life isn't good enough" messages with them into adulthood. The house can always be bigger, the paycheck larger. If I only had a boat or lived by the seashore or had married the elusive perfect mate I would be happier. The internal critic always wants more.

Some people understand God that way.

But not in this passage. This passage says it's not about sacrifices, it's about who we are in the world. In the next lines (Mic. 6:9–16), God announces that the only punishment is about social injustice. The passage reminds us it is not about building fires or killing animals or about riches or your job. It's about being a verb, not a noun.

It's about who we are at a very fundamental level and how we live in the world. The only thing God asks of you is to do your part to make the world a better place.

To love each other and do what is good in the world. To think of ourselves as walking with God, or goodness, in the world. To be a co-creator of a world that loves kindness and seeks justice. It could be in the little things you do today: picking up a piece of litter and throwing it away, doing an errand for a sick neighbor, bringing your co-worker a cup of coffee, sending a check to that organization you've been meaning to support, writing a letter to your Congressional Representative about a bill you read about in the newspaper.

Being, not wanting anything. Not demanding anything of ourselves but to be kind, forgiving and justice seeking.

Try imagining, or even better, believing that you are walking with a loving, benevolent God today who wants only for you to serve the world. What will you do differently today?

WHO IS A GOD LIKE YOU, PARDONING INIQUITY AND PASSING OVER THE TRANSGRESSION OF THE REMNANT OF YOUR POSSESSION? GOD DOES NOT RETAIN HIS ANGER FOREVER.... GOD WILL AGAIN HAVE COMPASSION UPON US.

Micah 7:18–19

I once gave a talk at a major university on sexuality and religion. At the end of the speech a teenage girl and her mother waited in the line where I was signing copies of my books until everyone else had left.

The (about) sixteen-year-old came forward and whispered, "Do you think God forgives the sins that people commit as teenagers?"

I asked her if she believed in a God of love and forgiveness. She answered "Yes." I told her I did too, and that I believed that there is nothing we could do—young or old—that would alienate us from God's love.

I wish I had remembered this passage from Micah in that moment. It not only doesn't imply that all people are sinners, but that God forgives people when they do sin and shows mercy and compassion to us.

Some of you have a different idea of sin than I do. My theology does not believe in original sin, the idea that all people are born as sinners, or that sin is transmitted by the very act of sex that brings us into being. I often talk about "original blessing" to illustrate that all of our births are miracles, beginning with a sexual act and hopefully conceived in a loving relationship. How different the history of religion might be if St. Augustine had conceived of "original blessing" rather than original sin! My own concept of sin is about broken relationships, causing suffering, and not honoring the gifts of life. Almost all faith traditions teach that there is always a possibility for love, healing and restored relationships.

This passage from Micah emphasizes healing, forgiveness and compassion from God. I also think it's a call to us not to stay angry, to forgive, to show mercy and have compassion for those who have angered, crossed or hurt us. It reminds us when we have been hurt by another to reach for compassion rather than return the anger.

My own senior minister, Rev. Frank Hall, often ends his service with these words from poet Miller Williams:

"Have compassion for everyone you meet even if they don't want it. What seems bad manners, an ill temper or cynicism is always a sign of things no ears have heard, no eyes have seen. You do not know what wars are going on down there where the spirit meets the bone."

I often remind myself of these words when I'm behind an angry passenger at the airport or a person who pushes me in the supermarket line or a driver who cuts me off cursing me because I'm driving the speed limit. I don't really know what is going on with them, so rather than responding with returned temper or ill manners,

I try to remind myself, "Compassion. I don't know what else is going on in their lives today."

It can even be with someone you think you know well. Perhaps a dear friend or even your spouse is insensitive to your feelings or rude or sarcastic to you. Before getting upset with him or her, it may be useful to ask what else happened that you don't know about. You could say something like, "You are usually so loving. I feel hurt (or angry) by what you just said, but I wonder what I don't know is going on in your life." I once had a major falling out with a dear friend. Months later, as we met to reestablish our friendship, we learned that we had both been going through deep stress during that time that we had taken out on each other. We chose to forgive each other and move on in order to reclaim our friendship.

A minister friend of mine taught me the spiritual practice of saying "fascinating." She told a story of one person blowing up at another person at a staff meeting and walking out of the room. The woman who was the recipient of the anger said aloud, "Fascinating," and continued on with the meeting. When my friend asked her how she could respond so neutrally, she explained that when faced with such situations, she had trained herself to say "fascinating" aloud and wonder with intention what could be going on behind the other's behavior.

What if for today, like God in the Micah passage above, you responded to every negative interaction with forgiveness, mercy and compassion? What if you trained yourself to think and say "fascinating" in such circumstances, being curious about what causes a person to act that way? How might that change your way of being in the world?

YOU ARE THE LIGHT OF THE WORLD. A CITY BUILT ON A HILL CANNOT BE HID. NO ONE AFTER LIGHTING A LAMP PUTS IT UNDER THE BUSHEL BASKET, BUT ON THE LAMPSTAND, AND IT GIVES LIGHT TO ALL IN THE HOUSE. IN THE SAME WAY, LET YOUR LIGHT SHINE BEFORE OTHERS, SO THAT THEY MAY SEE YOUR GOOD WORKS AND GIVE GLORY TO YOUR GOD IN HEAVEN.

Matthew 5:14–16

In the opening book of the New Testament, Jesus has been traveling through Galilee, teaching in synagogues and curing people of illnesses, demons, epilepsy, paralysis and pain. His fame is spreading as a healer, the text says, and enormous crowds are following him from great distances. As Matthew 5 starts, rather than addressing the crowds, Jesus climbs the mountain and sits down, and the disciples follow him. He begins to teach the twelve men the words of the nine Beatitudes (Matt. 5:3–12) and what we know as the Lord's Prayer (Matt. 6:9–15, also found in Luke 11:2–4). His voice and his words are heard down the hill where the people gather, and the crowds were "astounded at his teaching" (Matt. 7:28).

There are many wonderful passages in these few chapters, but the words in Matthew 5:14–16 speak to me most powerfully. "You are the light of the world . . . . Let your light shine."

Jesus isn't saying that to one person—he's saying it to all who can hear his words. We are the light of the world—each of us.

I don't know anyone who doesn't struggle with self-doubt, who doesn't at times wonder if they are good enough, smart enough, attractive enough, doing enough. Early on in my career, I often experienced what some have labeled "imposter syndrome", a feeling that I was enjoying success I had not earned, and that if someone scratched the surface, they would see that I didn't really know very much. At the first wedding ceremony I performed, I remember watching the flower girl and the bridesmaids enter and thinking to myself, "Where is the person who is going to marry them? Surely it's not me." I felt like I was playing dress-up in my new clerical robe.

These words remind us that every person has a light within himself or herself, and that light needs to be brought into the world. Every one of us has gifts that the world needs. Some have been blessed with the gifts of oratory, musical or artistic talents or the natural ability to organize others, and it can be easier for those lights to be recognized by the world. But maybe your light is different. Maybe you are a great parent, a great friend, a caring and kind person. Let your very particular light shine.

The world needs you to be everything you are, not less than you are. Despite everything in the commercialized world that helps make us feel "less than," this passage from the book of Matthew reminds us that we too are lights, and that we must not hide our gifts and our talents.

I'm sure you know the words to the beloved spiritual below. I'm singing the words as I type them. Join me:

"This little light of mine, I'm going to let it shine.
This little light of mine, I'm going to let it shine.
This little light of mine, I'm going to let it shine,
Let it shine, let it shine, let it shine."

Maybe close your eyes and sing it again, and feel your own light emerge. Take your light into the world today.

Do not worry about tomorrow, for tomorrow will bring worries of its own. Today's trouble is enough for today.

Matthew 6:34

I am a worrier. I come from a family of worriers. We don't just worry about tomorrow; we worry about what will happen next week, next month, and next year. I've learned as a minister that many people spend their lives ruminating endlessly "What if?" and "What's next?"

I love this passage because it reminds me that we can only live one day at a time. It's the Christian version of the Buddhist principle of not getting attached to the outcome.

When we are worried about a child, or an illness, or money, or our job, or our relationship, or the state of the world, we're often distressed about what will happen in the future. We create additional anxiety and stress by our ruminations rather than focusing on what we need to do to address the situation today. As someone once said, worrying about the future is like paying interest on a loan that may never come due.

This passage from the book of Matthew reminds us to pay attention to what is happening today. A wise older woman I knew said, "Dread one day at a time." During dark periods in our lives sometimes the best we can do is live one hour, even one minute to the next. But we don't have to live tomorrow's dark moments, especially because they may not come.

Know that you have the strength to deal with today's worries. Leave tomorrow's for tomorrow.

ASK, AND IT WILL BE GIVEN YOU; SEARCH, AND YOU WILL FIND; KNOCK, AND THE DOOR WILL BE OPENED FOR YOU. FOR EVERYONE WHO ASKS RECEIVES, AND EVERYONE WHO SEARCHES FINDS, AND FOR EVERYONE WHO KNOCKS, THE DOOR WILL BE OPENED.

Matthew 7:7–8

What a wonderfully optimistic passage this is! Jesus is teaching the disciples, and the crowds who are listening nearby, that it is through their actions that they can help shape their own lives. This verse is included in the Sermon on the Mount and comes after the Beatitudes and the Lord's Prayer. It is part of Jesus's instructions to the community. Like the Beatitudes, it is addressed specifically to the disciples although the crowds of people at the bottom of the mountain hear his counsel. Jesus is expressing his confidence in prayer and his certainty in God's response. He is also acknowledging that there are times when everyone needs to receive help from others.

Ask, seek, knock — and the doors will be opened.

There are those who proclaim what is known by some as the "Prosperity Gospel," that God answers all prayers directly. If we need money or riches or even a parking space, we need only pray for them. There are best-selling books that teach that the secret to success is asking God for favors, even riches, and that if one is pious enough, prayers will be fulfilled.

I personally find that interpretation of this passage cruel. People with incurable cancer will not get better simply through piety; people living in the most impoverished areas of the world are not failing to pray hard enough to relieve their need for food or health care.

Instead, I think this passage is asking us to pray but also to take matters into our own hands. A friend in Alcoholics Anonymous taught me that part of the wisdom of Bill W. is that if you're in a rowboat in the middle of the lake and it springs a leak, you pray to God but you must also row to shore. We are partners in our own salvation.

When we need help, we must ask ourselves what we need to do next. We often need to reach out to others and ask them to help us. When we are happy and things are going well, we must still look ahead and seek our future steps. Planning (seeking) and asking for help can both be important. We must not passively wait for prayers to be answered but open the doors ourselves, even if just a bit. We must knock at the doors of friends, physicians, counselors and neighbors for help when we know we can't fix things on our own. We can approach community agencies or faith communities that are new to us.

The passage reminds me of a parable that I heard a long time ago and that I have often used at the end of a speech or sermon.

It is a story that takes place in a small village a long, long time ago. In that village, like in every village a long time ago, there was a wise old woman whom the people in the town revered and who helped them with their problems and questions. The teenagers in that town, like teenagers ever since, doubted their elders and sought to discredit the wise old woman. The leader of the pack of teenagers came up with an idea.

"Let us go to the wise old woman with a bird in our hands. We will say to her, 'Wise woman, is the bird in our hands dead or alive?' If she says 'alive', we will crush the bird with our hands and show her the dead bird. If she says 'dead', we will open our hands, and the bird will fly away."

And with bird in hand they climbed the hill, went to the wise woman's home, and knocked on the door. When she came out, the leader said to her, "Wise woman, if you are so wise, is the bird in my hand dead or alive?"

She looked at them for a long, long time and was quiet, so quiet that the teenagers could barely stand still. And then she spoke, "The answer is in your hands."

It is in our hands. Whatever is troubling you right now, how could asking, seeking and knocking make a difference in your life?

If it is possible, let this cup pass from me; yet not what I want but what you want.

Matthew 26:39, Luke 22:42, Mark 14:36

Jesus knows the end is near. He has predicted that Peter will deny him three times, and that he is about to be betrayed. The text says he is "grieved and agitated" (Matt. 26:37). Jesus asks the disciples to stay away while he prays, and they are fast asleep each of the times he checks on them.

I believe we all have had times in the metaphorical Garden of Gethsemane. We too have felt alone, betrayed, denied and hopeless. It might be due to something in our workplace, in our family or marriage, with our friends. All of us know what it is like to be grieved and agitated, let down and alone.

And so what does Jesus do? He prays to God three times, with some version of these words: "Take this pain from me, take this burden from me, and please don't let me suffer like this." And then he says, "Not what I want, but what you want," or a few lines later, "If this cannot pass, your will be done."

It might seem odd that I've included this passage in a book about a hopeful view of God and our lives, but like the earlier passages in the Psalms and Ecclesiastes, I find the ideas in this passage comforting. Yes, life is suffering. None of us escapes that suffering; we all have times when life feels stressful or we feel alone, betrayed or denied.

Perhaps you have had a close friend turn on you unexpectedly. Or a colleague you counted on drops out of a project or takes a new job. Or a spouse tells you he or she is leaving you. Or a boss lets you know that your job will be eliminated. Perhaps life simply feels too overwhelming as you try to balance family, work, chores and time just to breathe. Although I've been fortunate to be married to the same man for the past thirty years, I've surely experienced the rest of these life-changing, out-of-my-control situations.

So where's the hope in this passage? It's that we are not alone and that everyone, even Jesus, knows what it means to despair. If we are theists, we can rest in God's love for us, knowing that it is not about us alone, that God is most with us precisely in these times of struggle. When I don't know what to do next or how to move from these moments of despair, I can remember that it is God who has brought me to this time and place, and that I must discern God's will for my next steps, my next decisions, for where I am to go from the Garden. God's will be done. For me, I can find comfort knowing, in today's lexicon, it's not all about me, but about God's will for me. And I can seek to be open to where that may be taking me.

But even if you are not a theist, this passage can speak to you metaphorically. We are not alone. We have family and friends who can support us. We can believe that our lives are unfolding as they are supposed to be. We can recognize that even in our times of great despair, it's "not all about me." And we can reach out for that support: Make a phone call, ask for help, reach out to someone we know we can count on, or do something nice for someone else. Sometimes at our lowest points, the best things we can do are volunteer or reach out to someone who is in worse shape than we are.

My colleague and friend Rev. Wayne Arnason wrote a short prayer that might work for you at these moments. I think he is praying a similar prayer to Jesus in the Garden:

> "Take courage, friends. The way is often hard, the path is never clear and the stakes are very high. Take courage. For deep down, there is another truth: You are not alone."

And what I say to you I say to all: Keep awake.

Mark 13:37

This passage from the Gospel of Mark is often the lectionary reading during the first week of Advent. In its own context, it was a call to the community to be watchful for the return of Jesus at the end of time. For many Christians today, Advent is a time to anticipate the miracle of the incarnation once again.

The call to "keep awake" is foundational to many religions. The word Buddha translates to the "Awakened One." There is a Buddhist legend which provides the background. A student meets the Buddha on the road, and recognizing something special about him, asks:

"My friend, what are you?
Are you a celestial being or a god?"

"No," says the Buddha.

"Well, then, are you some kind
of magician or wizard?"

Again the Buddha answers, "No."

"Are you a man?"

"No."

"Well, my friend, then what are you?"

The Buddha replies, "I am awake."

Being awake in the Buddhist tradition calls us to be fully alive, engaged and aware in the present moment. I've heard the principles of Buddhism described with these four simple statements that I try to use to guide my daily life:

Show up.

Speak the truth.

Do what you do with enthusiasm.

Don't get attached to the outcome.

Show up. This means being fully present, but it also means being available. Visiting a sick neighbor or fellow congregant in the hospital. Going to the evening meeting at your church or child's school. Calling your aging mother on the phone. Being present to other people. Not being distracted by your own wandering thoughts, but being fully engaged in the current moment.

Speak the truth. This is more than tell the truth. It means understand your personal beliefs and values, and share them. Resist the temptation to embellish stories or mask your own feelings and reactions. Be honest.

Do what you do with enthusiasm. Whatever we do, we can bring our whole selves to the interaction or project. Whether it's washing the dishes or tackling a new work project, we should approach the task with our most engaged selves. Life is not to be wasted, and as the

Ecclesiastes passage states earlier, we are called to be happy. Be fully present—in Mark's words, "keep awake" to the possibilities around you.

Don't get attached to the outcome. For me, and for many people, the last of this list is the hardest. My friends will tell you that I can be controlling, and that I like to plan my life to minimize drama and surprises. I want things to turn out well, whether it is with my family, a vacation or our organization. Buddhism teaches that a lack of attachment is the way to relieve suffering in life. It is especially at moments of greatest change or challenge that we need to do the first three—show up, speak the truth, do what you do with enthusiasm—and trust that the rest will work out. Graduation, a new job, falling in love, moving, retiring, having a baby are all moments of great change in our lives when we most show up, do it with enthusiasm, and not get attached to the outcome. Sometimes we just need to trust that all will be well.

We cannot hope to be like Jesus or Buddha, but we can reflect on them as exemplars for our own lives. We can seek to be more awake, more engaged in our daily lives. We can work to quiet our minds and distracting thoughts and bring our full attention to each other.

What would it mean for you to "keep awake" just for today? Life is calling all of us to do so.

I GIVE YOU A NEW COMMANDMENT, THAT YOU LOVE ONE ANOTHER. JUST AS I HAVE LOVED YOU, YOU ALSO SHOULD LOVE ONE ANOTHER. BY THIS EVERYONE WILL KNOW THAT YOU ARE MY DISCIPLES, IF YOU HAVE LOVE FOR ONE ANOTHER.

John 13:34–35

At this point in the narrative in the Gospel of John, Jesus knows the end is near. He has just washed his disciples' feet and foretold Judas's betrayal. Judas leaves the gathering, and Jesus tells the rest of the disciples that he will be with them only a little while longer. And then he offers them this new commandment, "Love one another."

Love one another.

But it's not really new at all. Jesus had been telling people this all along. He is cited as saying, "Love your neighbor as yourself" in three of the four gospels (Matt. 22:39, Mark 12:31, Luke 10:27) as part of the great commandment. (See the entry on page 14 for more). It is based in the Hebrew Bible in Leviticus 19:18: "You shall not take vengeance or bear a grudge against the sons of your own people, but you shall love your neighbor as yourself."

But here it's even more explicit, and it calls to us today in our own fast-paced, technologically-driven world. Love one another. Follow Jesus's many examples of unconditional love, acceptance and inclusion of the people around him. All the people, even and especially the most marginalized among us.

I find the intersection of my work as a sexologist and as a minister in these words. In both my professions, my work is to help people love each other with dignity, respect, acceptance and a radical sense of welcome to all.

Love one another. There is nothing more important than how we treat each other. Accept each other unconditionally. Bring our very best selves — not our tired, stressed out, too-much-to do selves — but our best selves to each of our interactions.

My friend Dr. Bob Selverstone, a marriage and family therapist, has a sign in his office that says, "Talk to me like someone you love." So often we can be crosser, more difficult with the people we love, using language or a tone of voice that we wouldn't ever use with strangers. Talk to the people you love only with words and tones that remind them of your love.

We all want to be loved. No matter how confident or how successful the person, inside each of us we wear a sign that says "Accept me for who I am. Tell me that I'm important to you. Notice me."

Jesus is telling us to accept each other just the way we are. He knows the disciples are imperfect; he's foreseen Peter's denial and Judas's betrayal, and yet he tells them simply: Have love for one another. Don't try to change each other. I love this portion of a poem from Hafiz, a 14th-century Persian mystic:

"Even after all these years,
the sun never says to the earth,
'You owe me.'
Look what a love like that does.
It lights up the entire sky."

For today, imagine that everyone you meet is wearing a sign that says, "Love me." Approach them knowing they are just as needy, just as insecure, just as lonely as you sometimes are. Accept them with grace and kindness as if you loved them, as if they love you.

The good news of this passage is that it's something everyone can do. We can love one another as God loves us. The even-better news of this passage is every one of us is deserving of being loved. Even you, today.

AND HOW IS IT THAT WE HEAR, EACH OF US, IN OUR OWN NATIVE LANGUAGE?

Acts 2:8

The story of the Pentecost is well known to many Christians. People of all kinds were "all together in one place" (Acts 2:1). The text tells us there were Galileans, Parthians, Medes, Flamites, Jews, Cretans and Arabs, as well as residents of Mesopotamia, Judea, Cappadocia, Pontus, Asia, Phrygia, Pamphylia, Egypt, Libya, Rome—it's the ancient world's description of the melting pot as they would have known it. The story tells us that suddenly all of these people heard a violent noise, and each began to speak in tongues and hear the word of God in their own language.

Picture if you will a day at the United Nations. People of all different nationalities are listening through headsets to translators who are relating the words of a speaker in another room. Everyone is hearing the same message at the same time in their own language. Except in the Acts story of Pentecost, there are no translators; it is just God speaking to each person in his or her own language, each hearing the same message of hope and salvation.

The passage is often preached on the first Sunday in June in many Christian churches. It is the story of how a large group of people came to follow Jesus after his death. But I view it as metaphor that speaks to my life.

It is a story of radical inclusion. People of all different lands, nationalities and ethnicities are gathered in "one place." They are separated by language, custom, and religion. They look differently, they dress differently, and they eat different foods. But something startling happens. Everyone receives the same message; no one is excluded. *No one.*

Perhaps that "one place" is not a single gathering spot, but earth itself. Perhaps we are all called to hear the same message, but each in our own way. The story reminds us that all people share the same wishes and dreams.

Do you know this hymn that many Christians and Unitarian Universalists sing, set to the music of Finlandia by Sibelius? It goes:

"This is my song, O God of all the nations,
A song of peace for lands afar and mine.
This is my home, the country where my heart is;
Here are my hopes, my dreams, my holy shrine;
But other hearts in other lands are beating
With hopes and dreams as true and high as mine."

For today, try to look at each person you encounter with a new perspective — the person at the coffee shop, the person who passes you on the street, your co-worker, the postal worker, your neighbor. They too want to be loved, to feel meaningful, to be happy and healthy, and not to be worried about money or their children or their health.

They want what you want. Take the time today to say hello and smile at everyone you meet. Include everyone, even the people who seem so different from you. It may just turn out to be a different type of day.

Awe came upon everyone.

Acts 2:43

Later on that Pentecost day, "awe came upon everyone," and all had the "goodwill of all the people" (Acts 2:47). No one is left out. All the people, no matter how different, receive the grace of being alive, of sharing the possibilities of being filled with reverence and the joy of living.

As I write this, the birds outside my window are singing different songs, some in their own robin language, some in their own wren language, some their own sparrow language. At first, I only hear it as birds singing, a single blended note. But when I slow down and really listen, the different songs emerge. I hear the robin, the sparrow and the wren individually. They are singing to their mates, but for right now, it feels like they are singing to me.

I look outside my window, and at first my mind only registers that there are tall green trees. But, as I slow myself down, I differentiate the evergreen, the pine, and the maple. I watch a bird fly from one to the other. By slowing down for a moment and really looking, really listening, I feel awe for the nature that I too often overlook.

The day is dawning, and I am given the gift of seeing today.

We have the opportunity to be awed, in our everyday surroundings, every day. Take a moment, right now, and look outside your window. Look, really look, at the nature that is right outside your window. Open your ears and listen, really listen. Take a deep breath and be in awe that you are created in a body that breathes for you without your needing to do anything at all.

Take a few minutes throughout today just to be and observe. Let today be a day, to paraphrase e.e cummings' words, when the ears of your ears awake and the eyes of your eyes are opened.

Your body is a temple of the Holy Spirit within you, which you have from God, and that you are not your own. For you were bought with a price; therefore glorify God in your body.

1 Corinthians 6:19–20

Paul is perhaps best known for his seemingly sex-negative comment, "it is better to marry than to be aflame with passion" (1 Cor. 7:9) or as many people know it, "it is better to marry than to burn." But just a few paragraphs earlier in the First Letter of Paul to the Corinthians, he has reminded the people of Corinth that their bodies are temples of the Holy Spirit and that they should glorify God in their bodies.

It's important to know a little bit about the city of Corinth at the time the Letter was written. Corinth was a thriving port city, also known as the City of Aphrodite; think of it as the Las Vegas of its time. Prostitution was common. The Christian community in Corinth believed that the end of time was coming, and they had written to Paul for his advice about sexual morality, including marriage, celibacy, divorce and the roles of men and women.

It is easy to think that perhaps Paul was extolling chastity and celibacy in this letter, but that is not how I read First Corinthians as a whole. Rather, Paul underscored that sexual relations are sacred and not to be engaged in lightly, for sexuality has the ability to affect one's life profoundly. Paul was urging the new Christians in Corinth to avoid using prostitutes—especially cultic prostitutes—because the physical act of intercourse involves the sanctity of becoming "one flesh" (1 Cor. 6:16). He allowed for adults to be both married and single, a radical notion for that time when the Roman law actually taxed bachelors and required widowed and divorced men to marry within a year.

Indeed, in the First Letter to the Corinthians, Paul explicitly recognized that adults experience sexual desire. The Letter acknowledges that people have the ability to make decisions about their sexual feelings, that sexual feelings are not uncontrollable, and that they should be acknowledged and acted upon only as they support one's values (1 Cor. 7:36–8). Indeed, in a surprising admission, he stated that his personal belief in celibacy was not from Jesus or God: "Now concerning virgins, I have no command of the Lord" (1 Cor. 7:25). It is clear that celibacy is not presented as a higher good.

Now, Paul clearly affirmed heterosexual marriage as the context for sexual relationships and emphasized the mutuality of roles, at least when it came to sex: "The husband should give to his wife her conjugal rights, and likewise the wife to her husband. For the wife does not have authority over her own body, but the husband does; likewise, the husband does not have authority over his own body, but the wife does" (Cor. 7:3–4). Further, partners have a right to expect sexual relations on a regular basis. It may surprise you to know that Paul wanted married couples to have sex: "Do not deprive one another except perhaps by agreement for a set time" (1 Cor. 7:5).

Despite our marked cultural differences from first-century Corinth and the belief that many of us hold that sexual relationships outside of heterosexual marriage can also be sacred, Paul's statements that our bodies are sacred, that sexuality is sacred and should not be treated carelessly, are still pertinent today. The Religious Declaration on Sexual Morality, Justice, and Healing, the foundational document of my organization, the Religious Institute, begins with the words, "Sexuality is God's life-giving and life-fulfilling gift.... Our faith traditions celebrate the goodness of creation, including our bodies and our sexuality. We sin when this sacred gift is abused or exploited." These statements are not so different from these passages from Paul.

How glorious it would be if our faith traditions had held up "your body as a temple" rather than "marry or burn" as Paul's central message about sexuality! What would it mean to think about your body as a temple, as a gift to you from the Holy? What would it mean to you to glorify the divine with your body? Might entering into sexual relationships or behaviors with an attitude of bringing the sacred into your midst subtly but powerfully change the nature of the experience? What if you and your partner prayed before and after sexual interactions, thanking God for the gift of your sexuality and your relationship? Try it and see.

LOVE IS PATIENT; LOVE IS KIND; LOVE IS NOT ENVIOUS OR BOASTFUL OR ARROGANT OR RUDE.... IT BEARS ALL THINGS, BELIEVES ALL THINGS, HOPES ALL THINGS, ENDURES ALL THINGS. LOVE NEVER ENDS.

1 Corinthians 13:4–8

Surely, you have heard these words read during wedding ceremonies. There was even a memorable scene in the movie "Wedding Crashers" in which there is a bet on whether they will be recited at the next wedding that the men plan to attend uninvited.

However, Paul did not write the First Letter to the Corinthians about romantic relationships. He was writing to a community struggling to understand how it needed to behave with the end of time so near. Love, he writes, is a gift from God, not just an emotion or human feeling. The Greek word for love in these passages is "agape:" God's unearned love for humans.

But there is a reason this passage is used so often at weddings, or as a reminder in church for all of us to act kindly toward each other. In the context of a new marriage, these words are perhaps best understood as aspirational, a goal to strive toward. It is our hope that the newly married couple will always be patient and kind toward one another, never rude or uncaring, and that the intense romantic love they feel for each other on their wedding day will not end until "death do us part."

But those of us in long-term relationships know that romantic love changes over time. Few long-term couples remain in the heightened days of overwhelming romantic love, but instead shift to a love characterized by their attachment for each other. Dr. Helen Fisher describes the three stages of love as lust, romantic love and attachment. Attachment, she writes in her wonderful book, *Why We Love*, is characterized by "the feelings of serenity and union with one's beloved."

In the day-to-day crucible of marriage, it is not easy to be our best selves with each other as we face the pressures of children, finances, aging, illnesses and so on. It is especially in difficult times that we need to remember these words from First Corinthians: Be patient. Be kind. Put up with what is currently distracting or distancing. Work so that love may endure.

When my children were little, I rebelled against teaching them through storybooks and Disney movies that they would fall in love, get married, and "live happily ever after." Instead, I would read, "they fell in love, they got married," and then I would substitute "it was a lot of work." Indeed, I believe that for any long-term relationship to last, whether marriage or friendship, that go-the-distance love, love that endures, requires a commitment to bring our best selves to each other, work through the struggles when we do not, and forgive ourselves and each other regularly.

This passage also calls us to bring love into the wider world—to love our neighbors as ourselves. And that perhaps is even harder. Paul is calling the Christian community of Corinth to love each other. Love endures because people commit to each other.

What if for the next week you take one quality of love out of this passage and intentionally work to manifest it in the world? Choose to have a day in which you practice patience, a day of kindness, a day without envy, and so on. Plan to have a day of hope in which you look at everything with optimism and anticipation of the good that is to come. Make love your inspiration for today.

FINALLY, BELOVED, WHATEVER IS TRUE, WHATEVER IS HONORABLE, WHATEVER IS JUST, WHATEVER IS PURE, WHATEVER IS PLEASING, WHATEVER IS COMMENDABLE, IF THERE IS ANY EXCELLENCE AND IF THERE IS ANYTHING WORTHY OF PRAISE, THINK ABOUT THESE THINGS.

Philippians 4:8

This may be my favorite passage in the New Testament. I used it as the final reading at my ordination ten years ago.

Our minds are so often cluttered. Our "to-do" lists cloud our minds. We may find it hard not to ruminate on things that are troubling us—a problematic co-worker, a fight with the boss, a call unreturned, a child who is not doing well.

We are too often bombarded with unpleasant images. I used to watch the local news before I went to bed. "If it bleeds, it leads" determines many local news shows. Car crashes, arrests, murders and war filled my late-night TV screen. They were not good images to have right before sleep or to dream about through the night.

The Philippians verse instead calls us to think about what is good, what is beautiful to the eye and the touch, what is just, what is excellent. It is a Bible passage that reminds us that the world around us is worthy of commendation and praise. We are asked to be thankful for that which seems to us true, honorable, excellent and pleasing. We can bring those images into our minds and allow them to fill us with joy.

There is research that demonstrates that keeping a daily gratitude journal can help students adjust to college and may help people who are depressed and grieving. Each night before I go to bed, I try taking the time to write down or remember three or more blessings I have encountered during the day. It is a way to remind myself that even on difficult days, life is good!

So for a moment, follow the advice in this passage. In the past few days, have you witnessed an act of justice or kindness to another person? What has pleased you or made you happy? What or who is worthy of praise in your life? Bring these images of the people and the goodness in your life into your mind. Shut your eyes and picture them. Let music and art and the people you love be the last images in your mind tonight. In your own words, offer praise for all that is "worthy of praise."

CLOTHE YOURSELVES WITH COMPASSION, KINDNESS, HUMILITY, MEEKNESS, AND PATIENCE.... ABOVE ALL, CLOTHE YOURSELVES WITH LOVE, WHICH BINDS EVERYTHING TOGETHER IN PERFECT HARMONY.

Colossians 3:12, 14

I was surprised to find these verses in The Letter of Paul to the Colossians. He is writing from jail, and speaking very specifically to the new Christians in the community of Colossae. Most scholars believe that an early disciple of Paul wrote the actual letter, but used Paul's name and story to frame the importance of responding to traditions that the author views as contrary to true Christian teachings.

The author tells the Christians in Colossae that they were once doing evil deeds and that they are to resist "philosophy" according to "human tradition, according to the elemental spirits of the universe" (Col. 2:8). He warns them that "fornication, impurity, passion, evil desire, and greed (which is idolatry)" will bring about "the wrath of God" (Col. 4:5–6). It's not exactly a letter that speaks to my Universalist heart or my belief that there are, as Rumi wrote, "hundreds of ways to kneel and kiss the ground."

But there are these wonderful lines of advice in the third chapter that do speak to me: "Clothe yourself with compassion, kindness, humility, meekness, and patience." What I find so compelling is that Paul isn't talking about treating *others* with compassion, kindness, humility and patience. We know there are many verses in Scripture which discuss how we are to treat our neighbor, the stranger and our family. Here, though, Paul is telling us we are to treat ourselves with the same care and consideration we know and offer to others.

I can imagine Paul (or his disciple) in his cell, not knowing how long he will be there, being kept from his work, feeling anything but patience and compassion for himself. Now, most of us haven't literally been to prison, but many of us have been imprisoned by physical or mental illness, by poverty, by jobs that don't fulfill us, by relationships that are destructive to us. How easy it is to beat up on ourselves in these situations: If only I weren't sick, anxious, or depressed; if only I had the courage to leave my job or my marriage; if only I were stronger than I really am. Our inner critic speaks to us stridently, in a much harsher tone than we use with anyone else.

On a more superficial level, I think about how I felt when I was beginning my yoga practice many years ago (not that I'm advanced now, either). I'd look around the room at the people in the perfect downward dogs, twists and headstands, and I would scold myself, "You aren't thin enough, flexible enough, young enough ever to be able to do this." I could look at the person on the mat next to me, also far from being in a perfect pose, and think kindly, "You must be a beginner like me." But somehow, I had a hard time turning off my own inner critic's much more severe messages.

On a much deeper level, I have, like most of us, struggled with myself, especially around illnesses and physical limitations that didn't heal quickly enough for me to get back to the work I feel called to do in the world. I can be a bit of a perfectionist, and goodness knows I struggle with patience. I have a magnet on my refrigerator, a gift from a friend that says, "Lord, give me patience...but please hurry."

When I am in that place, I sometimes stop and ask myself, "What would I say to a congregant or a client that came to me with a similar issue? How would I respond to someone waiting for the medicine to work, for the right job or contract to appear, whose financial situation meant they had to stay longer?" Without going into the actual words, I do know that I'd respond kindly and encourage him or her to be patient. I might remind them of those words by Julian of Norwich, the 14th-century English mystic, who was the first woman to write a book in English. She is perhaps best remembered for these words: "All shall be well, and all shall be well, and all manner of things shall be well."

In these passages Paul is reminding not just the people of Colossae, but I think reminding himself as well, to extend kindness, compassion and patience to themselves. Clothe yourself. Dress yourself, cover yourself in kindness. And remember that it is love—love for each other, but also self love and knowing that brings about "perfect harmony."

Just for today, let go of your inner critic. Let go of the voice that is hurrying toward tomorrow, six months from now, or next year. Treat yourself as you strive to treat others. Be kind and compassionate to yourself. What would it be like to have today be "perfect harmony?"

AND BE THANKFUL.

Colossians 3:15

It is curious that in the United States Thanksgiving is a single day set aside each year for people to give thanks. It is surely a Eurocentric holiday, even if many immigrants have adopted its customs and rituals. Few schoolchildren in the U.S. are taught that for Native Americans, it is a day of mourning of their losses at the hands of European settlers. But I admit that I enjoy our large, noisy family gathering with its traditional foods. And like many clergy, I use Thanksgiving as a theme for a service encouraging, as Paul does in this Letter, to "keep alert...with thanksgiving" (Col. 4:2).

I loved finding out that Meister Eckhart, a 13th-century mystic, wrote, "If the only prayer you ever say in your entire life is thank you, it will be enough." In this passage, Paul is saying similarly. Life is a gift, the world that God has created for us is a gift, and we are to be thankful.

When my children were small, we began a daily blessing that we have continued into their young adulthood. When we gather for a family dinner, we go around the table and each of us answers the question, "What am I thankful for today?" When my son was small, he most often said, "I'm thankful for the good day." It's a good answer for any of us.

We have so much to be thankful for. We can begin with the gift of our very lives—the miracle of a very particular sperm and egg uniting, surviving prenatally (nearly one in three conceptions is spontaneously miscarried), being born and surviving the first year of birth, of reaching whatever age we are today. If we are healthy, we can be thankful for our genetics, our resiliency, and the gift of our health, for we know it will not always be so. If we have a home, heat, electricity, and food to eat, we must be thankful, for so many people in the world do not. If we have people who love us who we in return love, we know how grateful we should be, for many people are alone. If we have work that pays us, and if we enjoy that work, we must consider ourselves blessed in a world where so many do not.

Stop and think right now: What do you have to be thankful for today? Make as long a list as you can. Consider the small things that came your way today—a smile from a stranger, a tasty bite of food, the sun on your face, and so on—and the big things that sustain you each day.

Take that attitude into today. Be alert to what makes you happy, what and who makes your life easier, what we need to remember is a gift to us. Be thankful—all day.

You must understand this, my beloved: let everyone be quick to listen, slow to speak, slow to anger.

James 1:19

I love the parts of the Bible that are common wisdom and still apply to people two thousand years later. They remind me that our human foibles are nothing new, but part of the essence of who we were created to be.

This passage lets us know that people have always failed to be good enough listeners, that they are quick to judgment and response and quick to anger. The hope in this passage is that we don't have to be this way, and we can remind ourselves of a better way of being with others in the world.

There is no greater gift we can give than listening, really listening, to another person. I learned a lot about listening when I was becoming a minister. I confess that prior to that I was often a person who, while listening to someone else, was thinking about how I might respond, how the story the person was telling me somehow related to my own life, and what I would tell them about me next. Even worse, if someone was upset with me, I would find myself fleeing into defensive mode, thinking about how if I could just help them understand me and my actions better, they would back down.

Then I read these words from St. Francis: "Grant

that I may not so much seek…to be understood, as to understand," or as James says here, "Be quick to listen, slow to speak." If my spouse or colleague or friend is upset with me, if I can be still and listen to their concerns and let them know that I have heard them, things often go better. I have sometimes been at meetings in which I know my judgment about something will be questioned, and have written on a piece of paper that only I can see, "Seek to understand, rather than be understood." It is a reminder not to become defensive and to listen — really listen — to others' concerns.

As part of the requirement for becoming a Unitarian Universalist minister, I had to spend 425 hours working as a hospital chaplain. It's a program called "Clinical Pastoral Education," known as CPE, and it was one of the best experiences of my life.

The very first day of CPE, we began working as chaplains, which meant going to visit patients in their hospital rooms without a prior invitation and asking them if they'd like to talk. Our supervisor told us that our goal was to talk as little as possible, but to give these patients the chance to talk to us. Now, I'm a problem solver *and* a talker, so I knew this was going to be a challenge for me.

But I'll never forget one of those first days walking into the room of a woman struggling with lung cancer room and saying, "Hi. I'm Debra, one of the chaplains here, and I wonder if you'd like to talk." Words tumbled out of her mouth, fears, regrets, a lost love, anger at herself that she had smoked and blamed herself for dying before she could see grandchildren. I held her hand and didn't say a thing, just listened attentively. At the end, spent, she looked at me and said, "Chaplain, that was wonderful. Thank you for what you just did."

And I thought to myself, "I didn't do anything." I hadn't even said anything.

But I had. She needed to talk, and I had listened to her. It was the beginning of a process of changing how I approached people in ministry and in my daily life.

The challenge is to bring this practice into our daily worlds. It can be harder to do that with a spouse or a friend or a co-worker, especially one who is upset with me. But what if instead of being defensive ("I did *not* forget to do the laundry!"), we really listened to the concern ("I feel like I'm doing more of the chores than you are and on a regular basis, and I'm tired of picking up after you"), and took responsibility for our role in making our partnership happier. Noted marriage and family therapist John Gottman advises that we remember that the goal of a fight in a committed relationship is not for one partner to win but to create a better relationship with each other.

Just for today, try it. Give one person your undivided attention and listen. Listen without thinking about your response. Take deep breaths and give yourself permission not to respond with your own story. Be quick to listen and slow to speak.

But someone will say, 'You have faith and I have works.' Show me your faith apart from your works, and I by my works will show you my faith.... Faith was brought to completion by the works.

James 2:18, 22

I like James the best of all of the Letter writers that come after the Gospels, and this verse especially resonates with me. It is not known to whom James wrote this general letter, although it says it is to the "twelve tribes in the Diaspora." Unlike many of Paul's letters, it is more general than specific in its topics, and it is more about God than Jesus. There is debate about who James is — some believe he was Jesus' brother; others write that he was a contemporary of Paul.

But this well-known passage couldn't be clearer or more direct: for James, righteous actions were more important than professed beliefs. More than 2000 years ago, people debated which was more important — having faith in God or how one behaves in the world. It is a debate people of different religions and indeed within religious traditions continue to have today.

I've had many evangelical Christians ask me if I've been born again. I've heard Christians worry aloud that

Jews or Muslims or Buddhists or atheists will never go to heaven, despite being ethical, worthwhile people, because they do not believe in the divinity of Jesus.

I once heard a very well-known person who had created a nationally known Christian service organization say in a public meeting, "I really worry about my Jewish friends, because no matter how good a person they are, they are going to hell." I gasped in horror, both as someone who comes from a Jewish background and as someone who is a both a capital "U" Universalist (part of the title of my religious affiliation) and a little "u" universalist (someone who believes that all people are interdependent.) I couldn't understand how a national leader who was doing such important work healing the world—and who had provided millions of opportunities for people to do volunteer work—could not only believe but publicly assert without blushing that anyone who wasn't a Christian would be condemned regardless of their character, relationships or contributions.

My own Unitarian Universalist tradition arose in response to theologian John Calvin, who taught that only some people will be saved and that the possibility of salvation is determined by God at birth; and in response to Martin Luther, who argued that salvation can come only through faith. 19th-century Universalist James Freeman Clark, in his paper "Five Points of the New Theology," responded to Calvin with the concept of "salvation by character"; in other words, like James, "works will show you my faith." Paul, in his Letter to the Ephesians, wrote similarly, "For we are what he has made us, created in Jesus Christ for good works" (Eph. 2:10).

It is not enough, as James says, to have faith and not

110

live a good life, but as he also writes later in this Letter, "Who is wise and understanding among you? Show by your good life that your works are done with gentleness born of wisdom" (Jas. 3:13). I understand "gentleness born" as showing kindness to others. The fundamental basis of my own theology is that there is nothing more important than how we treat each other.

We are also called to demonstrate our faith in the world through our "works"—our deeds, our actions, our kindness to others, our work for charity, how we serve others. I learned early on in my Jewish upbringing that we are called to leave the world a little bit better than the condition it was in on the day we were born.

In the Jewish tradition, there are three moral imperatives that encompass James's words: "mitzvah" or good deeds, "tikkun olam" or healing the world, and "gemilut hasidim" or acts of loving kindness. We are called to do what we can to help the world, to do good deeds for others, and to act lovingly. A mentor of mine, the late Dr. Sol Gordon, used to talk about "mitzvah therapy." There is no easier way to lift oneself out of a depressed mood or a bad day than to do something kind for someone else. Whether it's doing an errand for an elderly or infirm neighbor, reading to children at a school or doing volunteer hours at a soup kitchen (or any of the thousands of ways we can help other people), we are somehow lifted out of ourselves by volunteering for others and acts of kindness, and may feel better even if it is just temporarily.

Think about it. How do you bring your faith and love into the world through your words, your deeds, your actions? What one thing could you do today to demonstrate your faith through something you do? What mitzvah might you do for another person?

We often end the services in my home congregation with this quote from William Penn:

> "I expect to pass through this world but once. Any good therefore that I can do, or any kindness or abilities that I can show to any fellow creature, let me do it now. Let me not defer it or neglect it, for I shall not pass this way again."

What's one good thing you can do today?

WE LOVE BECAUSE GOD FIRST LOVED US. THOSE WHO SAY, 'I LOVE GOD,' AND HATE THEIR BROTHERS OR SISTERS, ARE LIARS; FOR THOSE WHO DO NOT LOVE A BROTHER OR SISTER WHOM THEY HAVE SEEN, CANNOT LOVE GOD WHOM THEY HAVE NOT SEEN. THE COMMANDMENT WE HAVE FROM HIM IS THIS: THOSE WHO LOVE GOD MUST LOVE THEIR BROTHERS AND SISTERS ALSO.

1 John 4:19–21

The First Letter from John emphasizes that people of faith love each other. The Letter was probably written at about the turn of the second century in response to a rift in that particular Christian community. Some had left the community, and the Letter writer was encouraging those remaining to stay committed to each other.

The love theme appears to come directly from the Gospel of John—"Love one another just as I have loved you"—but expands into the practical realm. The love spoken is not romantic or sexual love, but rather it is a call to offer unconditional regard and esteem to each other. Love is not a greeting card feeling in these verses, but rather a way of being toward other people.

The Letter reminds us that we have the capacity to love because God loved us. The verses caution that one cannot truly love God if one does not love other human beings. Historians understand that the Letter only applied to the believers in the Johannine community and not those who had left it, but I experience this passage as a much greater summons to care for all of God's creatures.

I love the challenge in the lines. How can you love the unseen God if you don't love the person standing right in front of you? If we are to be faithful to the spirit of God, or if you prefer, to the spirit of beneficence in the universe, we must love one another, take care of one another, offer compassion and welcome to one another. We must treat each other as God treats us — with unwelcoming regard and unconditional love. To do so is to act in the image of the divine.

This passage, both in its specific call and in its response to the schism in this early church community, reminds me of the dissension in many churches and denominations today about the full welcome of lesbian, gay, bisexual, transgender and queer people. These struggles have often been scarring, pitting neighbor against neighbor, and even splitting churches and parts of denominations. I can hear myself quoting this passage to those identify as Christian but do not welcome openly LGBTQ people in their churches or their pulpits: "If you love God, surely you must love all your brothers and sisters in the fullness of their own humanity." It is not enough in my mind to say that all are welcome but then work to disparage or even try to change people's sexual orientations and gender identities.

Loving and just faith communities welcome everyone. God has created sexual and gender diversity as one of God's blessings in the world, and we have an obligation to create a world that embraces the diversity of creation. This Letter also reminds us to stay in community while we work through our disagreements and differences.

It is not easy to love one another, most especially when we disagree strongly. I have a Brian Andreas painting above my desk that reads, "Anyone can slay a dragon," he told me, "but try waking up and loving the world all over again. That's what takes a real hero." I think that's what John was saying here as well. Love one another especially when it is most difficult. It could apply to your family, your spouse, your colleagues, or that rude person in the grocery store line. Approach the world with an attitude of love.

What would it mean today for us to approach all we meet as members of our own family? How might we love one another as God loves us? What one action could we take today to seek justice for others, whether it is people who live in poverty, who are immigrants, who are children without adequate food or health care, LGBT people and so on? Could we decide to treat each person we meet today with an open heart, with compassion, and kindness? How might that make today a better day, or the world a better world?

Let's try it and see.

LET ANYONE WHO HAS AN EAR LISTEN TO WHAT THE SPIRIT IS SAYING TO THE CHURCHES.

Revelation 3:13

The book of The Revelation to John, known more widely as Revelation, is a dark vision of the apocalypse, filled with angels, beasts, dragons, locusts, horses, kings, plagues and blood. It contains bizarre, fantastic, scary images of a doomed world to come, in which only the believers are saved.

It is not a comforting book or indeed familiar to a 21st-century reader, and it is not often preached or even discussed in most progressive churches.

But I thought it fitting to close this book of good news with the above verse. Because I do believe, as the slogan from the United Church of Christ says, "God is still speaking." Or, as 20th-century comedian Gracie Allen is said to have said, "Never put a period where God has put a comma."

The Spirit is still speaking to us. It is speaking in the increasing role that women are playing as equals in religious communities. It is speaking in the increasing inclusion of lesbian, gay, bisexual and transgender persons in the mainline and progressive church, synagogue and mosque. It is speaking in renewed efforts to keep children safe, both in congregations and from clergy sexual misconduct, sexual harassment and abuse. It is speaking in the prophetic voices of those who are working for social and sexual justice.

The Spirit is still speaking in our own personal lives, if we can only have ears to listen. Take time each day to listen to the silence. Take time each day to listen to the beauty of the earth's sounds and music. Take time each day to listen to words of love and comfort from others. Take time to listen to what the Spirit is saying to you.

Peace and blessings on your journey.

For More Information

If this book inspired you to take a closer look at the Bible, may I suggest that you might enjoy some of the books that have taught me on my journey:

Buehrens, John. (2004). *Understanding the Bible: An Introduction for Skeptics, Seekers, and Religious Liberals.* Boston: Beacon Press.

Gomes, Peter J. (2002). *The Good Book: Reading the Bible with Mind and Heart.* NY: HarperOne.

Kugel, James L. (1999). *The Bible As It Was.* Cambridge: Belknap Press of Harvard University Press.

Shelby Spong, John. (2009). *The Sins of Scripture: Exposing the Bible's Texts of Hate to Reveal the God of Love.* NY: Harper One.

About the Author

The Rev. Debra W. Haffner is an ordained Unitarian Universalist minister and an AASECT certified sexuality educator. She is the co-founder, President and CEO of the Religious Institute. This is her seventh book.

About the Religious Institute

The Religious Institute was founded in 2001 as a multi-faith organization advocating for sexual health, education and justice in America's faith communities and society. More than 6000 religious leaders from more than 70 faith traditions are part of its network. For more information, visit religiousinstitute.org

PERSONAL REFLECTIONS

Personal Reflections

PERSONAL REFLECTIONS

Made in the USA
Charleston, SC
18 January 2013